Chinese Chess

This is a Carlton Books

Chinese calligraphy based on the work of Du Zhong Xing,
President of the Xi'an Calligraphy Association.

Text, design and illustrations © Carlton Books Limited 2000

1 3 5 7 9 10 8 6 4 2

A CIP catalogue for this book is available from the British
Library.

UK edition ISBN 1 84222 102 7
USA edition ISBN 1 84222 040 3

Project Editor: Vanessa Daubney
Project Art Direction: Gavin Tyler
Design: Vaseem Bhatti
Production: Lisa French

Printed and bound in China

Chinese Chess

James Palmer

CARLTON
BOOKS

Contents

Xiangqi   6

The Rules   8

The Differences
between Xiangqi and Chess   22

Troops and Terrain   32

Opening the Game   46

Tactics   60

Endgame   82

Dirty Tricks   102

Sample Game   108

Cultural Background   118

Further Information   124

Xiangqi

THIS BOOK IS an introduction and tutorial for the ancient game of Chinese chess, called xiangqi in Mandarin Chinese. It is intended both for people familiar with Western chess (henceforth referred to simply as chess) who wish to explore a fascinating variant, and for those who have never played any version of chess before in their lives. The later chapters should also be of some interest for more experienced players as they contain discussions of advanced strategic techniques. Each chapter has been given a heading from Sun Tzu's The Art of War, a classic text which applies well to xiangqi.

Chapter 1 is a simple summary of all the rules of xiangqi for easy reference purposes. If you are familiar with Western chess, then you might want to skip straight to Chapter 2, which focuses on the differences between the two games. You should read Chapter 1 at some later point, to make sure you are totally clear on the rules of the game. Chapter 3 details basic strategy and has more details as to the specific roles of each piece.

Using the board and diagrams provided, you can try out various techniques and positions as you go along, but the best way of learning the game is always to find somebody to play against! If you do not have a suitable opponent, details on xiangqi clubs are included on page 124, as well as some Internet sites where you can find an opponent. By the way, you might notice that some of the early problems have far fewer pieces than you would expect of a real game, including leaving out the Red and Black Kings. This is in order to make the initial problems simpler and more understandable; later problems are more realistic and complicated.

Chapters 4 through 7 go into more detail on difficult rules and the role of each of the pieces, and detail sample strategies and tactical moves that you might want to experiment with. You might well find Chapter 7 particularly useful at first, as it contains a range of useful tricks to play on an opponent, especially one who is more familiar with chess than xiangqi. It is best to play through a few games yourself before you tackle the sample game in Chapter 8, or it will make very little sense tactically. Once you are familiar with the basic strategies of the game, though, it acts as an excellent introduction to more cunning techniques.

Sample problems are given at the end of most chapters. Chapter 9 contains a range of tougher problems, for which only hints, not solutions, are provided. Finally, Chapter 10 details the history and current culture of the game, and suggests further reading and ways to contact other players.

The Rules

Xiangqi is, in essence, a model of a small war. Each side has a King, who commands various troops with differing abilities. Capturing this King wins the war, but to do so you must penetrate your opponent's defences, counter his attacks, whittle down his forces and finally capture the King in his Palace.

The basic rules of the game are very simple. There are two sides, Blue and Red. Each player takes it in turn to move one of his pieces, each of which moves in a different way along the intersections of the board. No piece (except the Cannon) can ever move through or jump over another. If you move one of your pieces to an intersection occupied by one of your opponent's pieces, your opponent's piece is captured and removed permanently from the gameboard. Red always makes the first move.

The aim of the game is to place your opponent's chief piece, his king, in a position where he cannot possibly escape capture. This is known in English as checkmate, or sometimes just mate. The King is a very weak piece, but is central to the game.

> Remember that play takes place on the intersections of the lines, not in the squares.

Terrain

The gameboard has three notable terrain features, which are central to the game. The first is the River in the centre of the board. This divides the board into two territories. Some pieces cannot leave your territory, while others gain additional powers when in your opponent's territory.

THE RIVER

THE RED PALACE

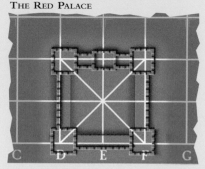

As well as the River, there are two Palaces, one for each side. Each of these is a three by three grid with a cross inside. Two pieces, the Advisor and the King, cannot leave their own Palace, and exploiting this limitation is very important for checkmate purposes.

Pieces

There are seven pieces in xiangqi, each of which moves in a unique fashion. Each is represented by a counter bearing a particular Chinese character. It is slightly confusing to find that the Red pieces do not always bear the same character as equivalent Blue pieces. For example, if you look at the characters for the Red and Blue Advisors, you will find that they are not the same. This makes no difference at all to the way the pieces behave during play. To make identification easier, common Western symbols for the pieces have been provided on the other side, and you might want to play with this side face-up at first.

The King

The King (*Jiang*) is the most important piece in the game because, if your King is captured, you have lost. It is a weak piece in itself, however, because it can only move one point at a time, horizontally or vertically, and only within the Palace, as diagram 3

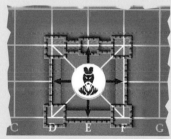

THE KING'S MOVE 3

shows. Each side has only one King. The King has one special limitation; you cannot make a move that would result in the two Kings facing each other, with no pieces in between. This is known as a King Confrontation and is discussed in more detail on page 83.

The Advisor

The Advisor (*shì*) acts as defensive cover for the King. As with the King, it can only move inside the Palace, one point at a time. Unlike the King, it moves diagonally, along the lines of the cross, as diagram 6 shows. Each side has two Advisors.

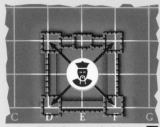

THE ADVISOR'S MOVE 4

The Elephant

The Elephant (*xiang*) is also a defensive piece, but is more flexible than the Advisor. It can move two points at a time, diagonally, as seen in diagram 5. Here the circles indicate the points that the Elephant can move to. It cannot move just a single point; it must always move two. Also, it is unable to cross the river, and must always stay within its own territory. Each side has two Elephants.

If there is a piece in between it and its desired destination, whatever side that piece belongs to, the Elephant cannot move in that direction, nor can it capture the obstructing piece. Diagram 6 illustrates this. Here the Red Elephant cannot move to either of the points marked X, being blocked by a Blue Chariot on the left and a Red Pawn on the right.

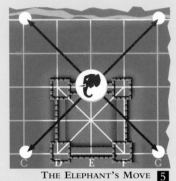

THE ELEPHANT'S MOVE 5

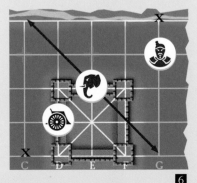

6

Blocking an Elephant in this way is known as blocking the elephant's eye.

The Horse

The Horse (*ma*) moves in a very odd way. Firstly, it moves one point either horizontally or vertically, then it moves another point diagonally, which must be away from their original position, not backwards. Diagram 7 illustrates this; the Red Horse can move to any of the circled points. Again, each side has two Horses.

Like the Elephants, the Horse can be blocked by any piece in between it and its destination, as diagram 8 shows. Here the Red Horse cannot move to any of the points marked X, as the Blue Pawn blocks its movement. This is known as blocking the horse's leg.

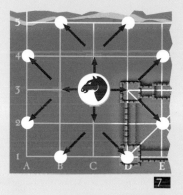

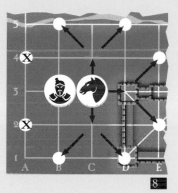

The Chariot

A nice simple piece, the Chariot (*ju*) can move any distance horizontally or vertically, as seen in diagram 9, where the Red Chariot can move to any of the circled points. It cannot move to a point if another piece is between it and its destination, as shown in diagram 10. Each side has two Chariots.

帥車炮馬兵將仕

11

相
車
砲
馬
卒
士
象

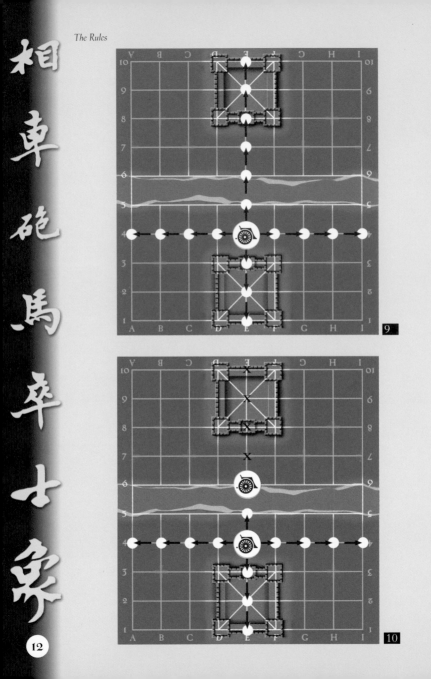

The Cannon

The Cannon (*pao*) moves in exactly the same way as the Chariot, as seen in diagram 11. However, it has a unique limitation and a unique advantage. It cannot capture pieces as other pieces do, simply by moving to their position. Instead, it must jump over another piece, belonging to either side, in order to capture. It is the only piece that can do this. Each side has two Cannon.

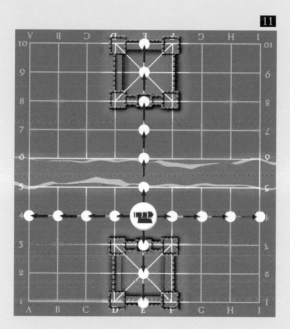

11

The Cannon's rules for capture are complicated, so look at diagram 12 closely. Here, the Red Cannon cannot capture the Blue Horse or the Blue Pawn, as there are no pieces between it and them. However, it can capture the marked Blue Cannon, by jumping over the Blue Pawn, or it can jump over the Red Chariot to take the marked Blue Pawn.

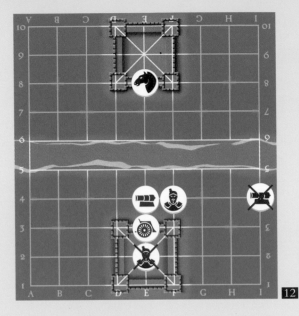

12

The Pawn

Pawns (*zu*) move one point forward at a time, and can never move backwards. If they move into your opponent's territory, they can also move a point right or left. In diagram 13, the marked Red Pawn has crossed the river into Blue's territory, so can now move horizontally. The unmarked Red Pawn is still in its own territory, however, so can only move forwards.

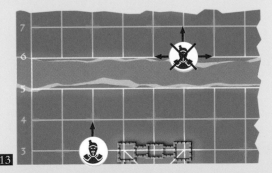

13

Winning the game

The game is over as soon as the King cannot escape being captured. Whenever the King is in a position where it might be captured, this is called check and the next move of the player whose King is threatened must be either to block or capture the piece that threatens check, or to move the King into a position where it is not in danger of capture. Diagram 14 shows this; here Blue must move one of his Advisors forward in order to block the Chariot's attack.

If there is no possible way for the King to avoid capture, this is check-mate (*jiang si*), and the King's player has lost the game.

Escaping check and threatening checkmate are discussed in much more detail in Chapter 4.

14

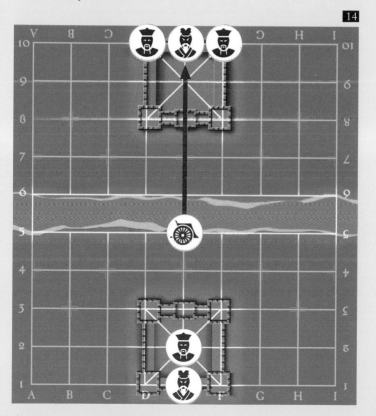

Setting up the board

Diagram 15 shows the starting positions, which are exactly the same for both sides.

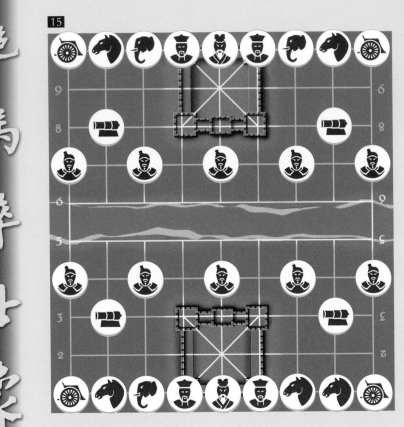

Algebraic notation

Xiangqi, like chess, often uses a system called algebraic notation to record the position of pieces. It records the location of a piece with simple co-ordinates, using A B C D E F G H I along the horizontal axis of the board from left to right, and 1 2 3 4 5 6 7 8 9 10 along the vertical axis from bottom to top. For instance, the Blue Horse in diagram 16 is on H8, whereas the Red King is on E2.

16

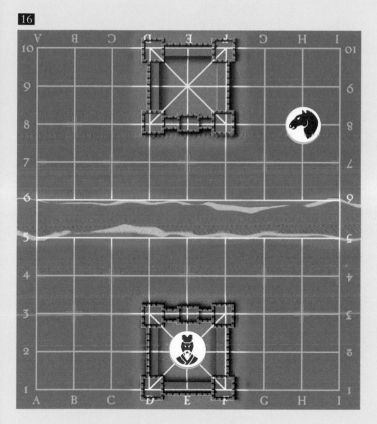

Problems

Each of these situations can result in Red capturing a piece. Which piece should Red move in order to do so, and how?

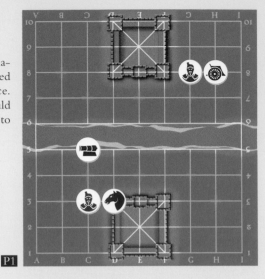

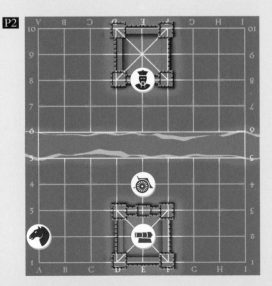

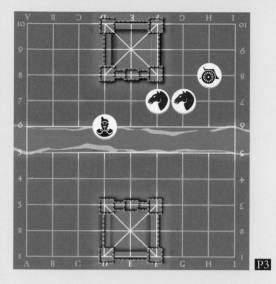

P3

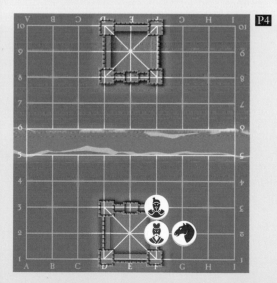

P4

帥車炮馬兵將仕

Solutions

The Red Pawn on G8 can take the marked Blue Chariot by moving a point to the right, as it is in enemy territory. The Red Pawn on C3, however, cannot do the same to the Blue Horse to its right, as it is still on its own half of the board.

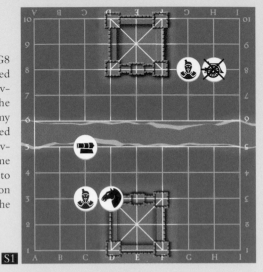

S1

S2

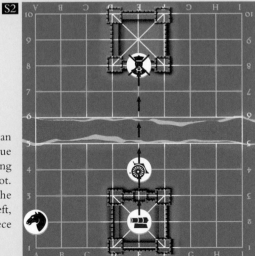

The Red Cannon can take the marked Blue Advisor by jumping over the Red Chariot. It cannot take the Blue Horse to its left, as there is no piece between it and the Horse.

20

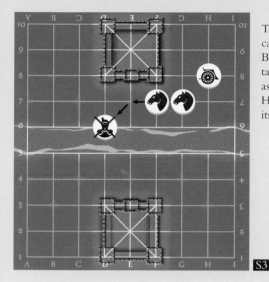

The Red Horse on F7 can take the marked Blue Pawn. It cannot take the Blue Chariot, as the other Red Horse blocks its movement.

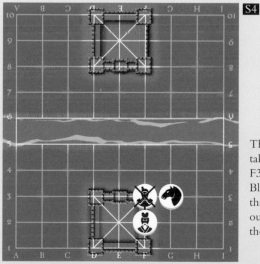

The Red King can take the Blue Pawn on F3. It cannot take the Blue Horse on G2, as that would move it outside the walls of the Palace.

帥車炮馬兵將仕

The Differences Between Xiangqi And Chess

If you are familiar with chess, xiangqi initially looks quite similar. Indeed, the aim of the game is exactly the same, to checkmate the King. However, there are a number of vital differences, and the feel of play is very different to chess. The difference between chess and xiangqi has been compared to the difference between a cavalry and infantry battle. Chess is free-flowing and sudden, xiangqi is up-close and bloody. It proceeds much more slowly than chess, and is dependent on rather subtler relationships between pieces. The King is considerably more vulnerable, and a great deal of attention must be paid to defence in order to ensure that your opponent does not make a sudden and deadly strike against your Palace. Pawns serve a quite different role, and Pawn structure is rather less important.

This chapter lays out the differences between chess and xiangqi, and is intended to introduce chess players to the game. You may well want to refer to Chapter 1, which lays out all the rules, in order to clarify some of the issues.

Let us start with the most obvious difference; play takes place on the intersections of the lines, the points, not within the squares, as shown in diagrams 1 and 2. Getting used to this is very important, as it is easy to slip back into thinking in terms of squares.

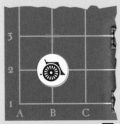

RIGHT **1**

WRONG **2**

Checkmate

Check and checkmate are exactly the same as in chess. However, there is no such thing as a stalemate. The exact rules for drawing games or losing through repeated moves are highly complicated and often disputed, but essentially, if one player repeats the same checking position three times, without changing which pieces are moved, he loses the game.

Terrain

The River in the middle of the board and the two Palaces at either end may look confusing, but really only serve as markers to limit the movement of certain pieces. The King and Advisor pieces cannot move outside the Palace, the Elephant cannot cross the River, and Pawns gain special powers once they have crossed the River into your opponent's territory.

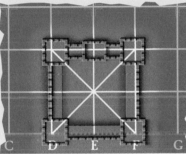

THE RED PALACE

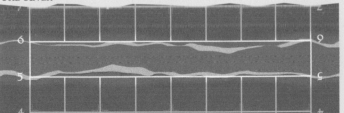

THE RIVER

The pieces compared to their chess 'equivalents'

There are seven pieces in xiangqi, as opposed to the six in chess. Many of them seem similar, but do not get complacent! Only one piece can really be said to have an exact equivalent in chess, the others all function in what might seem, at first, like very odd ways.

The King

As in chess, the King is the most vital piece in the game. The rules for check and checkmate are almost identical to those of chess, and we will not go into further detail until Chapter 4. Like the chess King, the xiangqi King (*jiang*) can only move one point at a time. Unlike the chess King, it can only move horizontally or vertically, not diagonally, as shown in diagram 6. Also, it can only move within the boundaries of the Palace, restricting it to a much smaller area than in chess and making checkmate considerably easier. There is no such thing as castling.

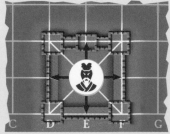

THE KING'S MOVE `6`

Finally, as noted previously, you cannot move your King into a position where it would face your opponent's King in a straight line across the board, without any pieces in between. This is called a King Confrontation and is a major element in many checkmates.

The Advisor

The Advisor (*shi*) has no real equivalent in chess. It is a limited defensive piece that moves exactly like the King, except diagonally rather than horizontally or vertically, as in diagram 8.

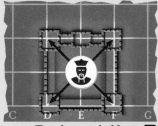

THE ADVISOR'S MOVE `8`

The Elephant

Very loosely speaking, the two Elephants (*xiang*) are equivalent to Bishops in chess. They move diagonally, but can only ever move two squares at a time, never less or more. They can never cross the river, and are always restricted to their side of the board. If there is a piece in between their starting point and their destination, they cannot move there. Preventing a move in this way is called blocking the elephant's eye.

The Horse

The Horse (*ma*) is deceptively similar to the Knight, and moves in exactly the same way. However, unlike the Knight, it is unable to jump over other pieces. If a piece blocks it, as shown in diagram 11, it is unable to move in that direction.

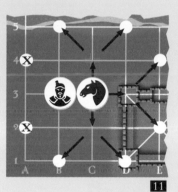

11

The Cannon

The Cannon (pao) is like a Rook (or the Chariot), except that it has a unique rule for capturing. In order to capture, a Cannon must jump over one other piece, belonging to either side, between it and its target. It is the only piece in the game that can jump, and it cannot capture without jumping. For instance, in diagram 12, the Red Cannon cannot capture the Blue Horse or the Blue Pawn on F4, as there are no pieces between it and them. However, it can capture the marked Blue Cannon, by jumping over the Blue Pawn, or it can jump over the Red Chariot to take the marked Blue Pawn on E2.

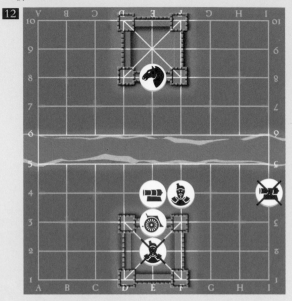

The Pawn

Another comfortingly familiar piece, the Pawn (*zu*) mainly moves in exactly the same way as the Pawn in chess, one point forward at a time. However, it can also capture by moving forwards and cannot move diagonally to capture, unlike the chess Pawn. It does not turn into another piece upon reaching the other side of the board, nor can it move two squares forward as its first move or perform en passant. However, it has one singular advantage which the chess Pawn lacks; upon crossing the river into your opponent's territory, it can move (and capture) one point horizontally, as well as vertically, as shown in diagram 14.

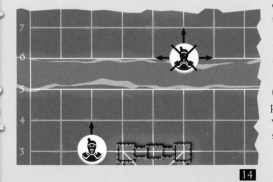

The Chariot

The Chariots (*ju*), you will be pleased to hear, are exactly like Rooks in every way, shape, and form. They move any distance, horizontally or vertically.

Setting up the board

Diagram 15 illustrates how to set up the board at the start of play. Red always makes the first move.

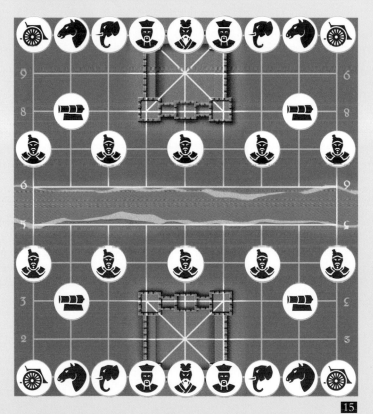

15

Problems

The following problems all illustrate the differences between chess and xiangqi.
Is this check or checkmate, and why?

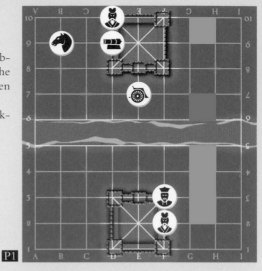

P1

P2

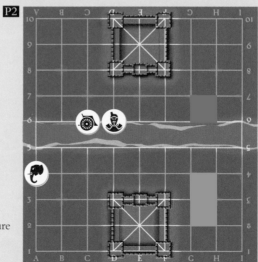

How can Red capture the Blue Chariot?

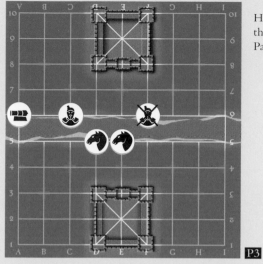

How can Red capture the marked Blue Pawn?

P3

P4

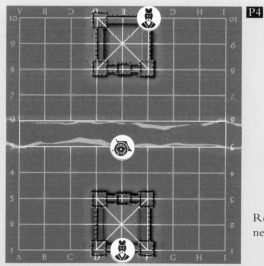

Red can checkmate next move. How?

帥 車 炮 馬 兵 將 仕

相
車
砲
馬
卒
士
象

Solutions

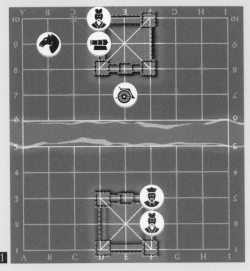

This is checkmate. In chess, the King would be able to move to the spot marked X, and it would be check. However, in xiangqi the King is unable to move outside the Palace walls, and so he is caught between the Chariot and the Horse. The Blue Cannon cannot take the Horse, as there is no piece in between them.

S1

S2

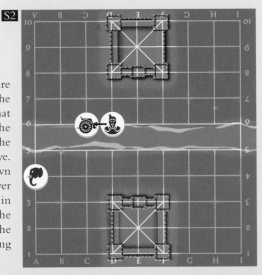

Red cannot capture the Chariot using the Elephant, as that would require the Elephant to cross the River, an illegal move. However, as the Pawn has crossed the River and is therefore in enemy territory, he can capture the Chariot by moving one point left.

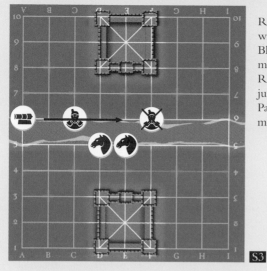

Red cannot capture with the Horse, as the Blue Horse blocks its move. However, the Red Cannon can jump the other Blue Pawn and capture the marked Pawn.

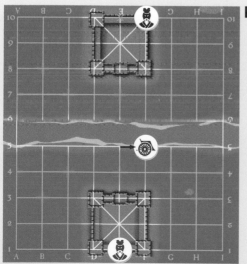

Red moves the Chariot a point right, checkmating. Blue cannot move to the spot marked X, as this would create a King Confrontation.

帥 車 炮 馬 兵 將 仕

31

Troops and Terrain

The rules of xiangqi on their own can seem a little intimidating, without the question of how to put all these different pieces to work. This chapter looks at the unique abilities and limitations of each of the pieces, and teaches some of the basics of xiangqi strategy. If you've played a game or two already, you've probably worked out some of these elements for yourself; if not, you might want to play a game with the help of these principles. All of these principles are elaborated upon in later chapters; this serves simply as an introduction to the general elements of tactical play.

The divisions of the board

Each of the ten ranks and nine files on the xiangqi board has a name, which also serves as a rough guide to which pieces you should be trying to place there. Diagram 1 shows the traditional names for each rank and file. Note that the divisions are, naturally, symmetrical. Your back rank is known as the base rank, and it is here that you should try and keep your King, naturally shielded by the initial set-up of pieces. Protecting this rank with a Chariot or a Cannon is often a sensible idea.

The second rank is the throat rank,

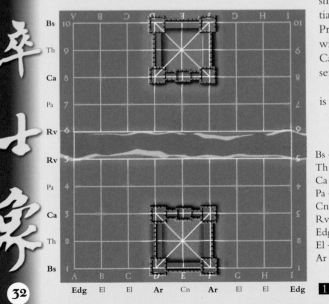

Bs – Base rank
Th – Throat rank
Ca – Cannon rank
Pa – Pawn rank
Cn – Central files
Rv – River bank
Edg – Edge files
El – Elbow files
Ar – Armpit files

so called because of its vulnerability. This is a dangerous area, as checkmates often take place when the King is forced here, so be wary of it, and defend it well.

The third rank is the Cannon rank. This is where the mustering of your army mainly takes place, and where you put together your Horses, Cannon, and Elephants into an effective attacking force.

The fourth rank is the Pawn rank. This is a very powerful rank for an attacker to control, so be cautious. In particular, an enemy Chariot or Horse here near the beginning of the game can do devastating damage.

The fifth rank is the river bank. Send your Chariots to control here, cutting off enemy Pawn invasions.

As for files, the central and fifth file is known as, well, the central file. Not everything gets to have an interesting name, unfortunately. This file is vital to the King's security, and should be the most heavily defended.

The fourth and six files are the armpit files, and, as they are in the Palace, are also important for the safety of the King. Use your Elephants and Advisors to defend them.

The second, third, seventh, and eighth files are the elbow files. A lot of movement takes place on these, as well as Pawn attacks, and it's a good idea to keep them open for your pieces.

The first and ninth files are the edge files. Chariot and Cannon attacks sometime take place along here, and the elbow files can be threatened from here. Generally, however, they are not as important as the other files.

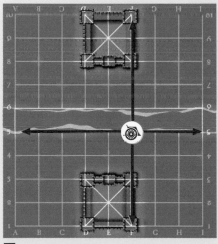

The four principles

There are four core principles that form the basis of any xiangqi strategy. These are Control, Support, Threaten, and Sacrifice. Learning how to utilise all four in unison is essential for good play. Further tactical variations will be explored in later chapters, building on these four principles.

Control

A central concept in both chess and xiangqi is having control over areas of the board. To have control over an area means that any opposition piece that moves there can immediately be taken by one of your pieces. For example, the Red Chariot in diagram 2 has control of both his river bank and the right-hand armpit file, effectively preventing unsupported Blue troops from moving onto either. In diagram 3 the Red Horse has control over all the spots marked X. Normally control is a great deal more limited than this, however, as the board is cluttered with pieces.

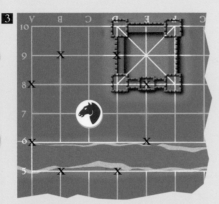

The more territory you control, the better. When your pieces are blocked in by each other, this cuts off their range of control. For example, in diagram 4 the Red Chariot is blocked by the Pawn immediately in front of it, preventing it from controlling the file, giving it control only over the throat rank. Clearly, it should be moved into the open as soon as possible.

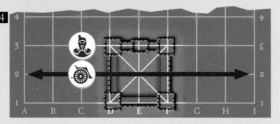

Support

Backing up the idea of control is that of support. If a piece is supported, it means that if it is captured, the opposition piece that captures it will immediately be captured itself. Look at diagram 5; here the Red Horse is supporting the Red Pawn and Cannon. The Blue Chariot could take either of them, but it would then immediately be taken itself.

34

Supporting your pieces allows you to move into territory controlled by your opponent, because if he takes your intruding piece, then he will be immediately captured himself and lose control of the territory. In diagram 6, the Blue Elephant controls C6 and G6. Red, however, can move a Pawn onto either of those spots without fear, as they can be supported by the Red Chariot, which would immediately take the Elephant if attacked. Note, however, that Red should avoid moving both Pawns forward together, as that would mean that the Elephant could take the Pawn on C6, as the Chariot would be blocked by the other Pawn and therefore unable to support it.

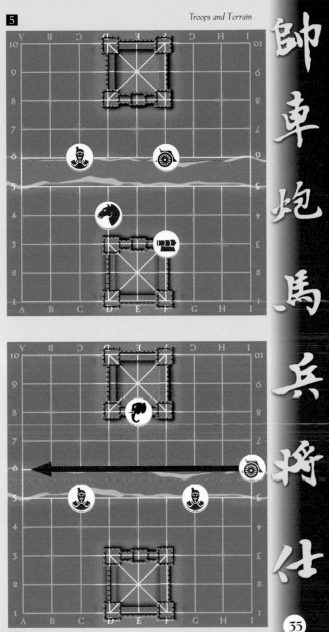

Threaten

Any piece that could, on your opponent's next move, be captured is said to be threatened. For example, the Red Cannon in diagram 7 threatens the Blue Horse. Threatening pieces is an important tactic both strategically and psychologically; if an opponent is aware of a threat to a valued piece he may concentrate over-much on that and ignore danger elsewhere. Moving

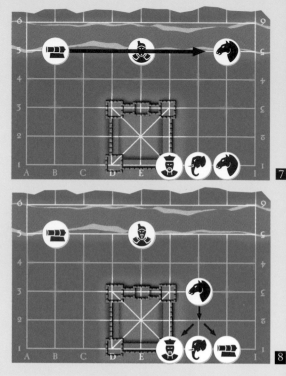

your pieces away from threats is very important, but try to attack rather than retreat. For instance, the Blue Horse in diagram 7 would be much better off moving to the position shown in diagram 8 rather than retreating, as this now creates a new threat to the troops on Red's base rank.

Sacrifice

It is often necessary to sacrifice a piece in order to gain a tactical advantage. One very obvious use of this is sacrificing a piece of lesser value so that you can take a more powerful enemy piece. For instance, in diagram 9, Red has just moved his Pawn forward as shown. This threatens Blue's Cannon and his Advisor, and so forces him to take the Pawn with his Chariot, allowing Red to take the Chariot with his Horse and incidentally threatening check on the King if the Advisor moves. The final position is shown in diagram 10. A straightforward double-capture, where both players lose a piece, is known as an exchange.

As a general guide as to when sacrificing a piece would gain an advantage, the Horse, Cannon, and Chariot are considered to be strong pieces, as they can be used for both attack and defence, and are the main ingredients in all checkmate scenarios. The Chariot is perhaps the strongest of these three, but it is a close run thing. Also, it is much better to have two different pieces left such as a Horse and a Cannon than to have two identical ones such as two Horses. If your opponent has left, say, only two Cannon and a Horse, and you have two Chariots and a Cannon, it would be greatly worth your while to sacrifice your Chariot in exchange for taking his Horse, as this would leave you in the stronger position.

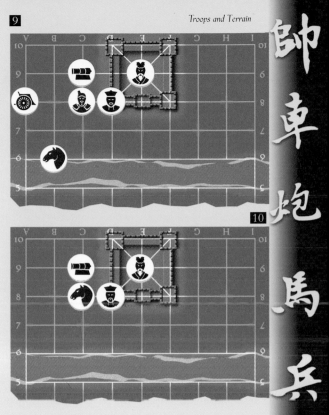

The Advisors and the Elephants, as they are purely defensive in function, are considered weak pieces. Sacrificing one of these in order to take a strong piece is almost always a good idea. In particular, getting rid of one of your Advisors can often be a good thing, as it gives your King more freedom.

The value of Pawns changes considerably depending upon their position. Before they cross the river and gain greater manoeuvrability, they are the weakest pieces in the game. Once they cross the river, they are probably worth about as much as an Elephant, but this varies greatly depending upon their position. For instance, a Pawn near the Palace is extremely powerful, much more so than one on the edge file.

The flow of the game

Rather than merely playing one move at a time, you should always have a definite plan that you are working towards. The best players always think several steps ahead, and have a firm short-time goal. For example, it might be control of the left hand side of the board, or the elimination of the opponent's Chariots. The worst type of play is simply to react to your opponent's moves; this gives him the advantage and means that, at best, you can merely defend against his attacks. Unless your opponent makes a serious mistake, reactive play will get you nowhere. At the same time, however, you should always be willing to modify your plan to new circumstances, or even, in extreme cases, to abandon it completely and quickly devise a new one.

The opening moves of the game are largely concerned with establishing your troops in good defensive positions, setting up attack formations, and generally getting ready to implement your strategy. Often, the first really aggressive moves in xiangqi only come after the twentieth move; before that, both sides are largely concerned with mustering their own forces. It can seem tempting to make an initial swift attack, especially with Cannon. However, this normally results in the loss of the unsupported attacking piece, plus an exploitable disturbance in your own defences. Diagram 11 shows a typical early attack, which, as it happened, eventually resulted in Red losing the game due to the crucial absence of his cannon, as shown in diagram 12.

In the middle game, the players jockey for position around the centre of the board, generally exchanging two or three pieces. Play can seem very tentative in xiangqi, as the defender normally has the advantage and attacks must be cautious; a slow gaining of territory and a set-up for a final attack is the normal technique. It is the midgame which really determines the game; after it, one player is often clearly on the defensive. A few moves can then determine the game as one player's earlier weaknesses are exploited. Sometimes, a careless player neglects to attend to his Palace, and an advantage in forces or position is turned around as his opponent forces a sudden checkmate due to the bad positioning of his King.

Once both sides have taken considerable losses, play moves into the endgame. Here both sides have only a few pieces left, and an advantage of a single piece can mean the difference between winning and losing. For example, a player with one more Chariot than his opponent has a sure-fire advantage. Occasionally both sides have offensive pieces clustered around their opponent's Palace, and winning can be a simple matter of who moves first.

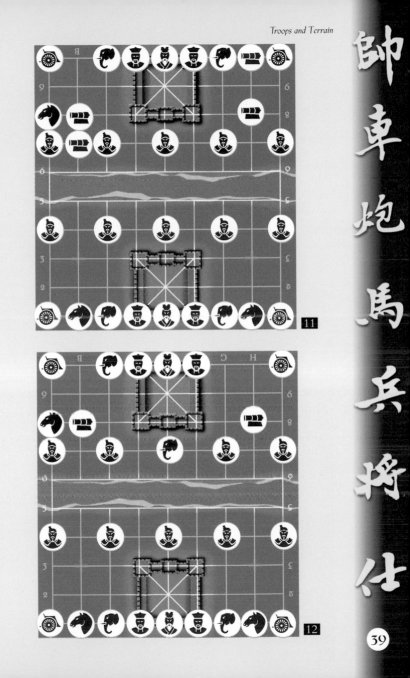

帥 車 炮 馬 兵 將 仕

11

12

The King and his Advisors

The most important piece in xiangqi, of course, is the King. It might seem at first as though the only purpose of moving the King is to escape from check. This is true to a certain extent; while the King is capable of capturing pieces, situations where this is possible are extremely rare, because the King lacks the relative mobility that he possesses in chess. However, the King does have one extremely powerful offensive power, the ability to exploit the rule of King Confrontation.

The King Confrontation rule states that the two Kings may never face each other in a straight line with no pieces in between. Effectively, this gives the King the relative power of a Chariot, but only for purposes of placing the other King in check – a very common way to force checkmate.

It is extremely important to keep your King working in conjunction with your Advisors. The foremost purpose of the Advisors is not to capture pieces, which their limited movement generally prevents, but to act as a screen for the King against King Confrontations. Capturing Advisors can be very useful, because having an Advisor or two when your opponent doesn't is a big advantage in exploiting King Confrontations. However, if you are in a position to capture an Advisor, you are often also in a position to checkmate.

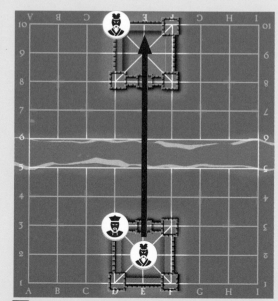

Look at diagram 13. Here the Blue King is prevented from moving to the spot marked X by the Red King, but the Red King can move to D2 if threatened, thanks to the shielding force of his Advisor directly in front of him. The weakness of this position, of course, is that if the Red King

13

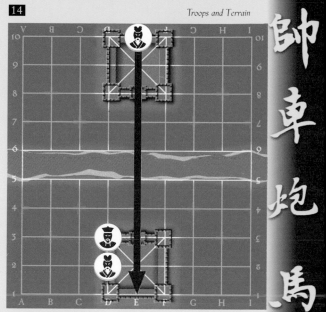

moves, the Blue King can immediately move to X and reclaim the central row, effectively reversing the positions, as shown in diagram 14. However, the Red Advisor can simply move to E3, thus shielding the King if he needs to move back. Consequently, Red's advantage in having an Advisor effectively gives him control of both Palaces.

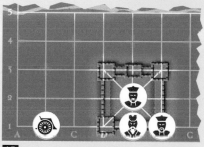

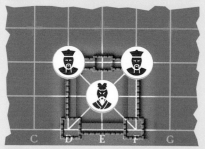

The disadvantage of Advisors is that they can block the progress of the King, preventing him from moving and allowing him to be easily checkmated, as shown in diagram 15, where the Advisors block the King from being able to escape the Blue Chariot. It is tempting to read some kind of ancient Chinese metaphor into this! In general, you should try and keep your Advisors at the front of the palace, as at the back they merely act as obstacles for the King. A good situation is shown in diagram 16, where the king's central position is a powerful tool for trapping his opposite number through Confrontations, while the Advisors act as a shield for him if threatened.

41

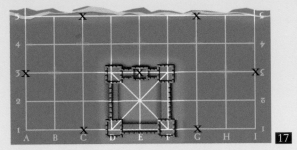

The Elephant

The Elephant is a very weak piece, due to its extremely restricted mobility, but it serves its purpose. There are only seven positions an Elephant can possibly occupy on the board, as marked in diagram 17. Ideally, you want to keep your Elephants on the Cannon rank, where they have the most control, as shown in diagram 18. Further forward, and they can only capture backwards, further backwards, and they can only capture forwards.

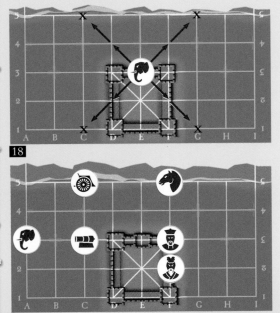

Elephants are often forgotten about, and can be a useful aid when the time is right. Look at diagram 19. Here the Blue player has failed to notice the Red Elephant, and his plan for forking the Cannon and Horse is about to be spoilt by having his Chariot taken.

The Horse

The Horse is an extremely useful piece, especially for capturing purposes. Its range of movement means that it can often fork two or more pieces, making it a splendid aggressive tool, and it is remarkably good at getting to the side of the Palace and checking the King. Diagram 20 shows a typical fork using the Red Horse.

The best way to defend against Horses is sometimes simply to block them. Even if you cannot capture a Horse, you can normally block its leg while at the same time setting up an advantageous position for yourself, and preparing to move another piece into a position where it can take the Horse. In diagram 21, the Red Horse is blocked by the Blue Cannon, preventing it taking the Blue Chariot, which can now move into a position to take the Horse unless it retreats. You

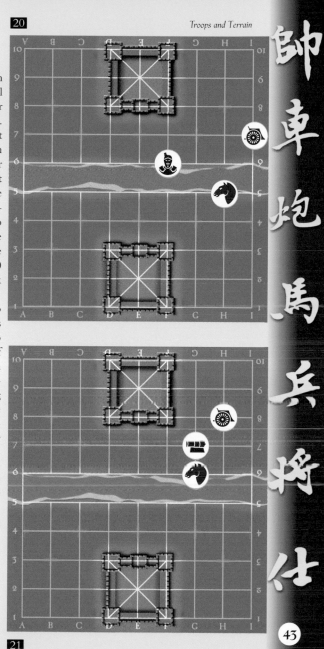

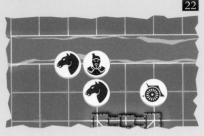

22

should be careful, too, not to block your own Horses. Remember that Horses are only blocked by a piece on one of the four points immediately next to them, not by pieces on the diagonals. The lower Red Horse in diagram 22 is blocked by the Blue Pawn from moving to the points marked X, but is not blocked by the Red Chariot or the other Red Horse.

The Chariot

Probably on average the strongest piece in the game, the Chariot has a versatility of movement that no other piece equals, and is capable of controlling great swathes of the board with ease. It is an essential ingredient in most checkmate plans.

As with Rooks in chess, the essential thing is to get your Chariots out from their starting position and unblocked by your other pieces, so that

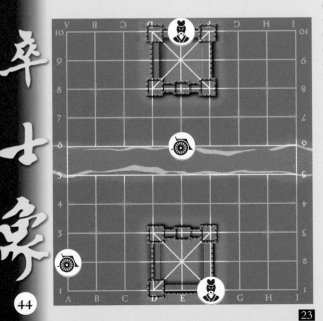

they can penetrate the enemy lines. A Chariot on an enemy file can be a dangerous piece. Use your Chariots to back each other up, each providing protection for the other.

As well as being very strong in attack, Chariots are extremely useful in defence, especially for preventing King Confrontations. In diagram 23, Blue would be able to force checkmate, but for the Red Char-

23

iot, which can move across and protect the King. A Chariot exchange would then result in a draw..

The Cannon

The Cannon is a complex but useful piece, particularly in the middle stages of the game, when the board is conveniently crowded with pieces for the Cannon to leap over. The most important thing to remember about the Cannon is its inability to capture without leaping; failing to remember this can lead to fatal mistakes. Let us clarify the

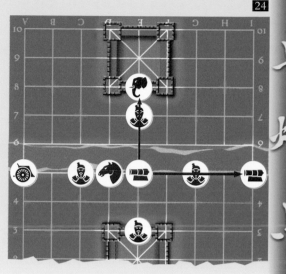

rules on capturing with the Cannon. You can only capture using a Cannon if only one piece is between you and your target. It does not matter who the pieces belong to. For example, in the completely implausible situation shown on diagram 24, the Red Cannon can capture either the Blue Cannon or the Blue Elephant. It cannot capture the Blue Pawn, because there are no pieces in between them, and it cannot capture the Blue Chariot, because there are too many pieces in between them.

The Pawn

The main point of the Pawn is slowly to advance your front line. Basic Pawn tactics, then, are to advance gradually, supported by other pieces who can take any stronger piece that captures the Pawn. Pawns are great pieces to sacrifice, and can be very threatening once they cross the river and gain the power to move horizontally. In particular, a Pawn just outside the enemy Palace is usable for certain checkmates, as we will see later.

Opening the Game

The opening of a xiangqi game sets the tempo for the whole battle. Will the game be fast or slow, a careful tactical skirmish or a reckless sacrificing of pieces on both sides? On which side will the players attack? What pieces will be at their forefront? Opening games vary widely, but there are some basic patterns which are often followed, and which this chapter will take you through.

Know your plan and your enemy

The most essential thing at this stage of the game is to be working towards a definite plan. Ideally, you should mentally sketch out the position you want after your tenth move before the game, and try to work towards that. However, your plan must naturally react to your opponents. Study each of his moves closely, and try to work out what his overall game strategy is. Be especially alert for weaknesses in his basic defensive structure, and try to distract him from noticing them.

Timing

Normally in xiangqi, you must strive to be one move ahead of your opponent, to force him to react to you rather than vice-versa, and a move that does not threaten your opponent in some way is largely a waste. In the opening game, however, you have considerably more latitude and, relatively unthreatened, can make moves that are little in themselves, but prepare for later stages of the game. As soon as your opponent threatens your pieces in any way, however, you should mentally switch to the normal way of thinking, where every move has to have an immediate impact.

Fast or slow?

The opening moves very much set the speed of the game. If both players stick within their own territory for the first ten or fifteen moves, then the game is likely to be a defensive one, quite probably ending in a draw, as neither player is willing to commit to a serious attack against the carefully established defences of their opponent. Early attacks produce a quite different game; one which moves rapidly away from the opening and into the midgame.

Either player can switch the speed from slow to fast, simply by making an attack. When to do this is one of the most difficult questions of the opening game. It is not enough simply to attack when you see an opportunity to take an enemy piece, normally a Pawn. Remember that an attack leaves one of your powerful pieces stuck in your opponent's territory where, at this stage of the game, he has all the advantages. Unless it is supported by other pieces, it is very easy for him to cut off and kill it.

Seize control

At the beginning of the game, your pieces have a very limited zone of control, even within your own territory. Your Chariots are stuck behind your Pawns, your Cannon are not supported enough to make attacks, and all your other pieces are restricted to the back row. Your Pawns, out in front, are totally unsupported, and a single Chariot stuck in that rank could scythe through them. Your initial objective, therefore, is to establish firm defensive control over your own territory.

There are some opening moves that are particularly effective in doing this – so common, in fact, as to be virtually, in one form or another, obligatory. These are tried-and-tested methods, and you will probably discover them to be the most effective forms yourself. On the other hand, players become so used to seeing and responding to them that you may find some unconventional technique to be an effective surprise tactic, but do not count on it.

Examining typical opening moves, we can also look at how the course of the game is likely to evolve from that point onwards. The first two or three moves of a game can often establish, for an experienced observer, where the later battles will be fought.

Central Cannon

The most popular single opening move, especially for Red, has always been shifting one of the Cannon to the central file, just behind one of your Pawns. This has several advantages: first, it provides control over the central file, thanks to the Pawn in front acting as a spotter. Second, it unblocks the elbow file the Cannon was on, letting you control it with other pieces later.

1

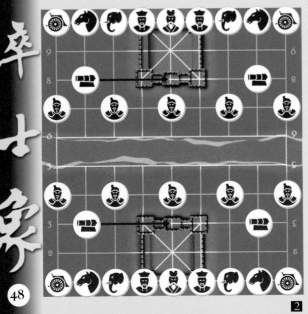

2

Third, it acts as a powerful threat to your opponent's King later in the game.

The normal response to this move is to move one of your own Cannon to the central file. You will find that many xiangqi opening games appear to have a strange reflective quality about them, as each side counters the other by performing exactly the same move! An important choice here is which of your Cannon to move in response. If you move the Cannon from the same side of the board, as shown in diagram 1, this is known as a same-direction Cannon opening, and indicates a fairly stable, likely defensive game. This is much more conventional than shifting your Cannon from the opposite side of the board, an opposite-direction Cannon opening, as in diagram 2, which creates a weakness on the flanks for both you and your oppo-

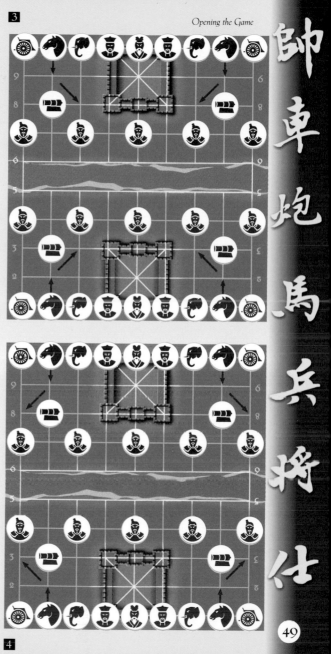

nent, and leaves you both vulnerable to a vicious counter-attack. Choosing this option is much riskier and means that early attacks on both sides are more viable.

Screen Horse

Another popular move in the opening game is shifting one or both of your Horses forward and towards the centre, as shown in diagram 3. Your Horses here form a screen in order to protect your Pawns, especially against a central cannon attack, to which this is a powerful and common counter. It also brings your Horses forward for later control of the river banks. This is a much more powerful opening than the other option for initial Horse movement, as seen in diagram 4, which gives you control over only one Pawn and pins your Horse uncomfortably against the side of the board.

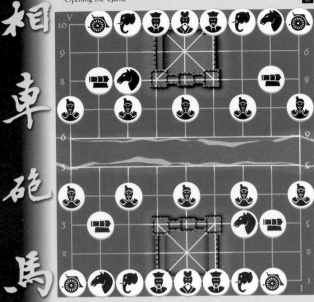

Filed Chariot

Another very common and powerful choice is the filed chariot opening, As we see in diagram 5, it begins with central Cannon and screen Horse moves, removing obstacles to the Chariot's movement, and then shifts the newly freed Chariot over a point into the outer elbow file. This gives the Chariot control over the file, which is very useful both for initial defence and possible later attacks, and supports it with the screened Horse.

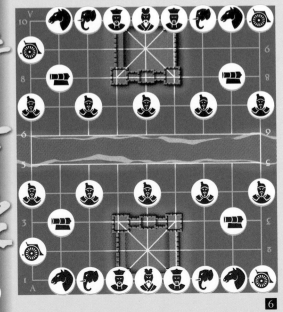

Ranked Chariot

A less frequent and more defensive move is simply shifting the Chariot forward to the throat rank, as in diagram 6. This lacks offensive potential, but provides a strong screen for the King. If your opponent is in the habit of launching strong attacks early in the game, you might want to experiment with this move.

A common opening

The most common and cautious opening sequence, therefore, is that shown in diagram 7: a central Cannon attack, Pawns protected by Horses, and Chariots on both sides in the edge files. You will probably find this set-up coming up a lot with inexperienced players! While strong, particularly defensively, it is also indicative of a certain conventionality of play, meaning that a good early attack will probably disconcert your opponent. Another slight variation on it, focusing on the central Cannon attack, is shown in diagram 8.

Accordingly, once you have played a couple of games, you might want to experiment with more interesting variations. Diagram 9 shows a variation popular in the 1970s, where, rather than using a filed Chariot, Blue instead advances a Pawn. This may seem a less powerful move, but gives him an initial advantage in seizing control of the river banks, as well as giving a little more flexibility in bringing out the Chariot later in the game. This is known as a Slowed Chariot opening.

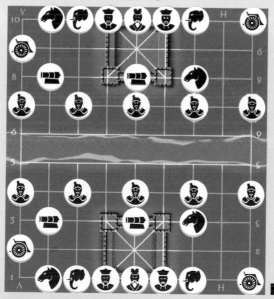

7

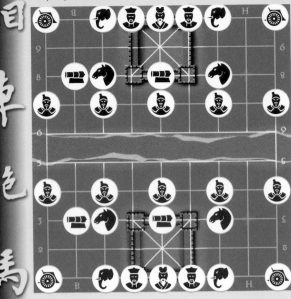

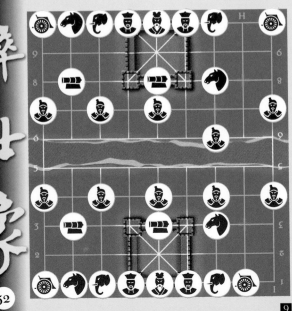

Another intriguing variation is moving the Cannon to the Palace corner rather than the centre file and supporting it with Horses, as shown by Blue in diagram 10. This is known as a Horse Sandwich. While not as initially threatening as the central cannon opening, this comes into its own at the beginning of the midgame, where the position of the Cannon has been proved to work well defensively against a conventional central attack.

Finally, another useful opening can be the Patrolling Chariot. An aggressively defensive position, if that is not a contradiction in terms, this brings the Chariot up to patrol the river banks, preventing enemy Pawns from advancing, as we can see in diagram 11. While it gives control over both a rank and a file, and is an excellent screen against Pawns, it is quite possible for a sensible opponent to simply support his Pawns with more powerful pieces, thus meaning that the Chariot in turn has to be supported, and often leading to an exchange of several pieces in the centre of the board. This move also leaves the patrolling Chariot somewhat vulnerable to a concerted enemy attack at the beginning of the game.

Early attacks

Knowing when to attack is one of the most important parts of opening play. The hallmarks of a successful early attack are that it both targets a weak spot in the opponent's ranks and is sufficiently supported that the attacking piece cannot simply be isolated and destroyed. It is also important to make the attack at the right time, preferably within the first few moves, throwing your enemy's tempo off and forcing him sud-

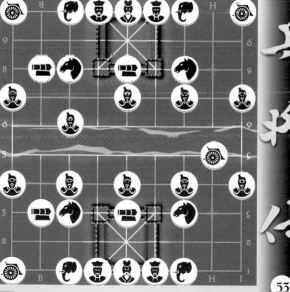

denly onto the defensive, which can disrupt his play for the rest of the game.

A typical effective opening attack is shown in diagram 12. Here Red has made the initial foray, bringing his Chariot forward into the Pawn Rank and threatening several Blue Pieces as well as taking a Blue Pawn, while at the same time supporting it with his Horses. Blue's best option here is to attempt a counterattack, threatening Red's supporting Horses rather than the Chariot itself.

Doubled cannon

Many early attacks utilize two Cannon. This is a strong combination of pieces because one Cannon can move up to act as a spotter for the other, especially when an enemy piece has been moved away to prevent this, but also acting as a threat in itself using the initial attacker as a spotter.

A typical set-up for an early Cannon attack is shown in diagram 13, where both Cannons are brought to the centre to threaten a strong open-

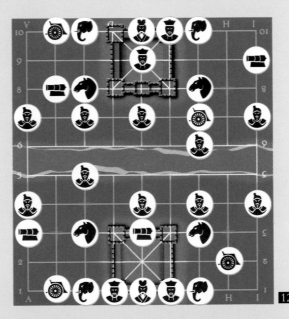

ing attack. Here the intention may in fact be to focus Blue's attention on the centre through the blatancy of the attack, and thus distract him from a later flank attack with Chariots and Horses, a cunning tactic. Alternatively, it can just serve as a blunt and powerful attack, if something of a sledge-hammer, and likely to result in several casualties in the middle of the board.

Diagram 14 shows a strong Blue attack using both Cannon, this time approaching from different sides rather than attacking together directly. This attack is particularly effective because both Cannon can support each other, as well as being backed up by Blue's Chariots, and so Blue gains control of a great swathe of Red territory. Red's most effective counter here is probably to try and sacrifice an Elephant or Horse to attract one of the Blue Cannon away from their threatening joint position on the Pawn Rank.

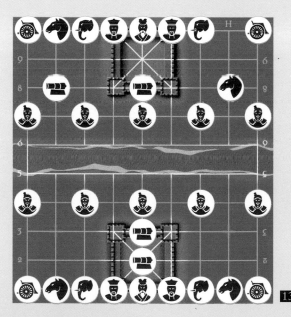

13

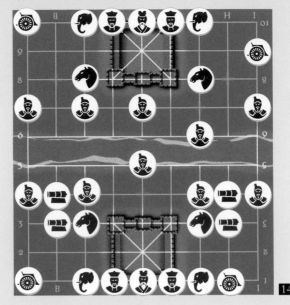

14

Two exchanges

There are two very obvious ways to exchange pieces at the beginning of the game. Generally, this is best avoided, but if you are certain that you do not want to use those pieces, and suspect that your opponent does, then they might be worth trying.

The first can be performed from the opening set-up, if you really want to, and is to simply take the enemy's Horse, sacrificing your Cannon in exchange, as shown in diagram 15. This is normally pretty dumb, as a Cannon is worth marginally more than a Horse and it allows your opponent to move his Chariot into a better position. It can be worthwhile, however, if it traps your opponent's Chariot behind his Cannon and you can then pin it with another piece. The game in the *Sample Game* contains a fine example of using this exchange properly.

Another possible exchange, if both players are using filed Chariots, is to take your opponent's Chariot with yours, having it taken by your enemy's Horse in exchange, as demonstrated in diagram 16. This is generally considered a dull move as it weakens both sides' offensive capacities, meaning the game will likely be longer and be more likely to result in a draw. On the other hand, it also forces your opponent's Horse back, weakening his central position and making an attack there more viable.

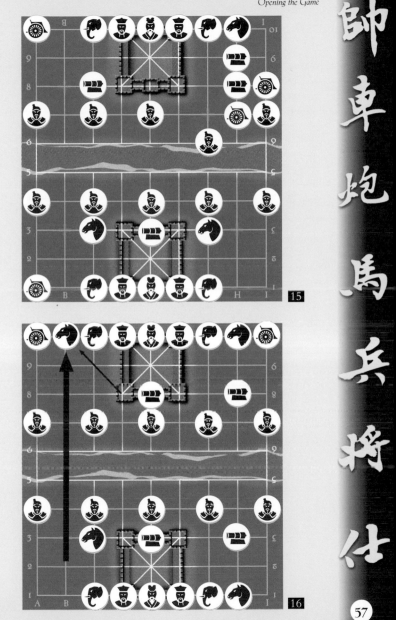

15

16

帥車炮馬兵將仕

The really strange openings

There are some openings, developed over thousands of years of xiangqi play, which are, to be honest, just plain bizarre and are, quite rightly, known as strange openings. The chief advantage of these is that they rather confuse your opponent, and often have possibilities that are not visible at first glance. The disadvantage is that they are, well, quite odd, and require a certain flexibility of mind to use, often sacrificing strong positions for slightly weaker ones that rely upon surprise and stealth for their effectiveness.

A typical strange opening is the tortoise-shell opening, as used by Blue and shown in diagram 17. This clusters pieces around the Palace, and can serve as a very effective defence against the central Cannon attack and a good set-up for a counterattack, unless Red knows the counter for it, which we see in diagram 18, in which case it becomes a very weak position. You will doubtless discover and experiment with many strange openings yourself, but be aware of their risks once your opponent works out their weakness; they are often only worth using once.

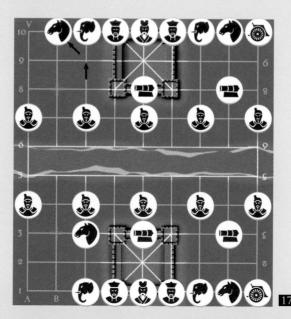

17

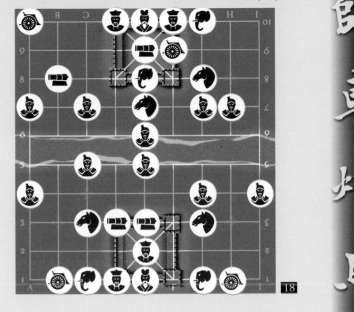

18

帥車炮馬兵將仕

Tactics

The xiangqi midgame is probably the most vicious part of the game. This is where both sides really see conflict for the first time, and pieces tend to get captured right, left, and centre. During the midgame, you have two main aims: to attempt a sudden checkmate, as always, and to end up with the most pieces in the endgame. There is no real set definition for the length of the midgame; it might end up as being anywhere between ten and fifty moves for both sides.

Initiate, do not respond

Critical to winning the midgame is being the attacker, rather than the defender. You should constantly attempt to be the aggressor. Your opponent should always be one move behind you, forced to react to your moves rather than initiating any of his own. Every move you make, even if defensive, should in some way threaten your opponent as well, or you will lose the initiative. Obviously, Red begins with the initiative, going first, but this can be easily lost. A purely defensive move, or one made just because you have to move, is a sure-fire way of losing the initiative, and will quite possibly lose you the game.

Be cautious, however, about being overconfident. Remember that the most threatening move is often one that supports another piece. Really great players, too, can convince their opponents that they have the initiative while, in fact, setting up their own attack. They seem purely to respond to their opponent's attacks, but a single move will then reveal all the previous ones as part of an intricate plan for checkmate.

The centre is a death-trap

The centre of the board is a killing ground, particularly points E5 and E6. More pieces are taken here than anywhere else on the board. If you attack here, therefore, you are upping the ante, and both sides are likely to take significant losses. If you have got a clear plan which only utilizes one or two offensive pieces, or you want to move the game faster towards the endgame, then attacking in the centre is a good idea. Otherwise, be aware that you will probably lose the piece you are attacking with, and more besides, and consider attacking your opponent's flanks instead.

Make sacrifices

In xiangqi, your overall position is far more important than the number of pieces you have. Unless both sides are down to very few pieces, it is generally worthwhile sacrificing a piece in order to gain a positional advantage. Many tactical tricks rely on sacrifice, especially of pieces that your opponent is particularly eager to take. Do not throw your troops away, but be prepared to lose them where necessary. Remember that a seemingly equal exchange can actually hurt one side far more than the other. If you are losing the game badly, you want to make as many exchanges of offensive pieces as possible, because every piece your opponent loses increases the chance of a draw.

Advance your pawns

Moving your Pawns forward continually is always a good idea. If you cannot think of anything else to do, march a Pawn towards the enemy ranks. Not only do Pawns become three times as powerful once they have crossed the River, they also serve as valuable support for your other attacking pieces, and act as thorns in the side of your opponent. If he is distracted by clearing up Pawns from his territory, you can force an attack elsewhere. Once in your opponent's territory, start bringing your Pawns closer to your enemy's Palace, setting up a mutual network of support between them.

Knock out supporting units

Quite often you will find that you are prevented from making a vital move because your opponent has the point you want to occupy controlled or the piece you want to capture supported. In this case, move your attention from the original target to the enemy piece that is supporting it, and attack that instead. Capture or force away the supporting piece, and you can then take your original objective.

The counterpart of this is that the best defensive structures are circular – piece A protects piece B which protects piece C which protects piece A. In this case, there is no weak point that can be targeted by your opponent, and any attack must result in capture.

The best defence is a good attack

The header pretty much says it all, really. It is normally bad play to react to an enemy attack by simply moving threatened pieces out of the way. In the case of a crowded board, you are only opening up new areas for him to attack. If the board is emptier, he can probably just chase you around the battlefield until the piece is taken. Kings are especially restricted in their ability to retreat, being so tightly confined to the walls of the Palace. Instead, when you are attacked or checked, you should react by attacking in return.

The best counterattack is checking your opponent's King. This immediately puts him on the defensive, and allows you to take back control of the game, later eliminating the original threatening piece. Second best is threatening the attacking piece, especially with a doubled attack on one of your opponent's defending pieces. Threatening uninvolved pieces sometimes works, but only if they are of sufficient value to your opponent that he will call off the attack to stop them being taken. Otherwise, you will simply move into a rapid culling of pieces on both sides, and since your opponent made the first move, he will come out ahead.

Doubled attack

One of the best moves of the midgame is the doubled attack, or fork. This move consists of simultaneously threatening two of your opponent's pieces with a single one of your own, meaning that, whatever he does short of capturing the threatening piece, he must lose a piece. For example, the Red Chariot in diagram 1 has forked the Blue Pawn and Horse.

Horses, because of their peculiar movement pattern, are often particularly useful for forking pieces, as is shown in diagram 2. Here Red has a distinct advantage, and unless Blue acts quickly and decisively, will be able to choose whether to attack by tak-

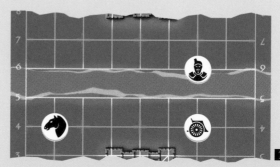

1

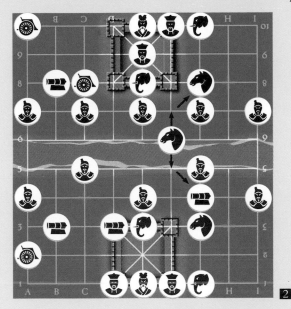

2

ing the Blue Horse, or remove the possible threat from the Blue Cannon. You might notice here, too, that while the Red Horse can take the Blue Horse, the reverse is not true, because the Blue Horse is blocked by the Pawn in front of it.

Doubled attacks in xiangqi are often rather long, a series of moves that eventually force your opponent into sacrificing the right piece. For example, the Red Chariot in diagrams 3 to 8 initially moves to threaten the Blue Advisor and Horse. Blue responds by threatening the Chariot with the Horse, but Red moves down and threatens Blue's Cannon, forcing it to retreat. Red then moves up again, threatening Blue's Pawn and Cannon. Blue then attempts to move his King out of danger, but Red forces it to retreat, and finally takes Blue's Cannon.

Doubled attacks are very powerful and versatile. The best response to them is to use the move in between your opponent's threat and his capture of one of your pieces to initiate a counterattack of your own. You will lose one of your pieces, but will have gained the initiative.

相車砲馬卒士象

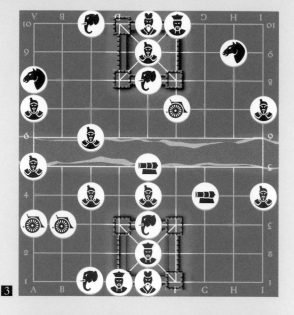

3

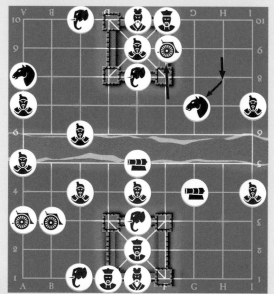

4

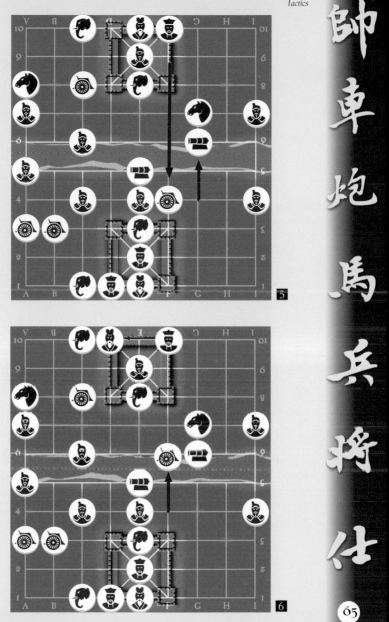

相車砲馬卒士象

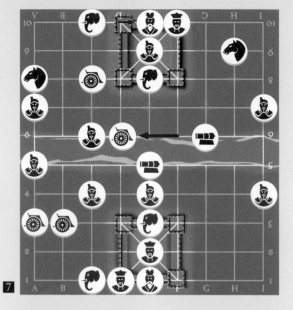

7

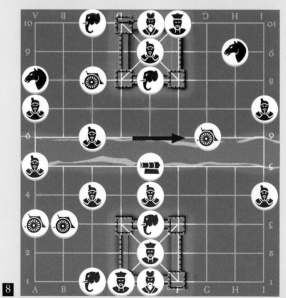

8

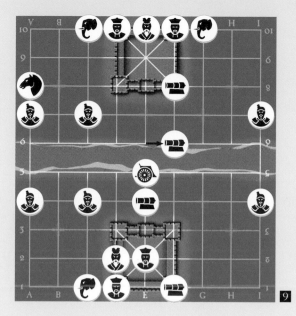

Side-step

Another common tactic is the side-step. This means that you threaten your opponent not with the piece that you move, but with the piece immediately behind it, freeing up a blocked piece, in effect. Even better is if the piece you move goes into a threatening position, effectively attacking your opponent on two fronts. Diagram 9 shows an effective side-step, freeing Red's Chariot to check the King and threatening Blue's Cannon with the second Cannon on the back row at the same time. Side-steps involving Cannon, oddly enough, often involve moving a second piece in front of the Cannon, so that the Cannon can jump it and attack. Particularly effective is piling two Cannon together, so that after the attack, the Cannon that was previously in front can then jump and attack a second enemy piece.

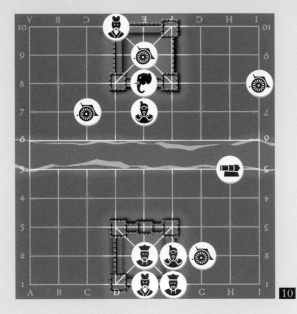

Attract

Luring your enemy into making moves for you is always useful. Attempting to attract a piece means that you sacrifice one of your own pieces, or simply place it temptingly open to attack, in order to attract an enemy piece into a dangerous or useless position. Preferably, the piece you sacrifice will, on its initial move, threaten the piece you want to attack. This means that your opponent has no choice in the matter; he must either take the piece and lose his later or lose it straightaway, without the advantage of having taken one of your pieces. This tactic is especially useful when used in conjunction with checking, as this can literally force your opponent to move the piece you wish to attract.

For example, diagrams 10 to 12 show a situation in which both sides are threatening mate. Red sacrifices one of his Chariots in order to lure the Blue King into a more passive position, allowing him to threaten it with the second Chariot and forestall a Blue checkmate.

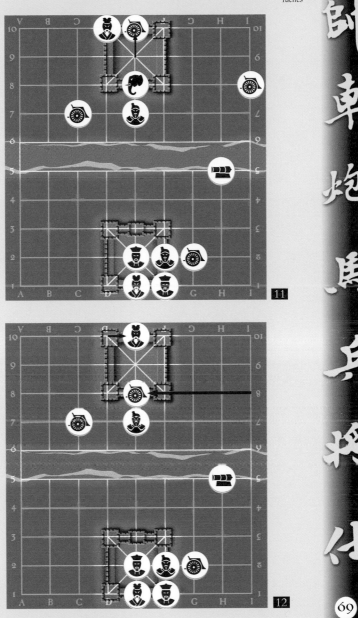

帥車炮馬兵將仕

相車砲馬卒士象

Lure away

Attracting enemy pieces away from a position that they guard is another good trick. Much the same principles apply to this as to just attracting a piece, except that the follow-up attack is directed not against the lured piece, but against the newly vulnerable area or piece it was guarding. For example, diagram 13 shows a situation where the Blue King is currently well guarded by his two Advisors. In order to facilitate an attack, Red therefore has to take the Advisor on D10 with his Chariot, meaning it is in turn taken by the other Advisor, as shown in diagram 14. Normally, this would be a bad exchange from Red's point of view, but here it serves to open up space for an attack on the Blue King by Red's Pawn and second Chariot.

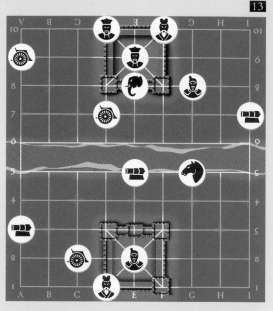

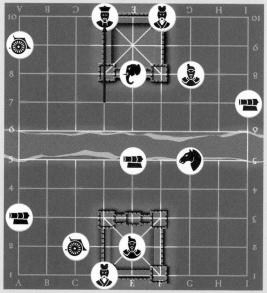

Whittle down

A very common pattern in the midgame is that both sides build up care-ful defences, networks of support that ensure that no piece can be taken without the attacker being captured in return, and then boom! somebody makes an attack, the defences of both sides swing into action, and several pieces get taken in a row. Sometimes this is an accident, but sometimes it is a good idea deliberately to trigger this kind of massacre, sacrificing sev-eral pieces on both sides. Whenever you notice multiple pieces supporting and threatening a particular point, this is an opportunity to start whittling down both sides.

When doing this, you want to make sure that you are the aggressor, who generally comes out a piece ahead, even if only a minor one, and you also want to be certain that your later battle plan can go ahead with only a few pieces. Once started, this process is almost impossible to stop, as neither side can afford to call it off. Diagram 15 shows a typical set-up just before this tactic is used. In this case, both sides have their Horses trained on the Blue Pawn on E7.

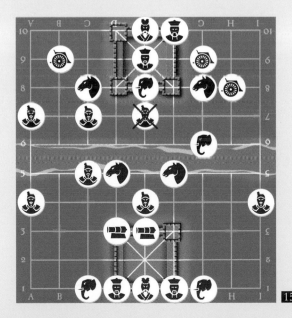

15

As soon as Red moves to take it, there's an inevitable sequence of captures, it does not particularly matter in which order, finally resulting in the loss of all four Horses. Red, however, comes out ahead, thanks both to now being a Pawn ahead and to having moved his Chariot into a better position, as we see in diagram 16.

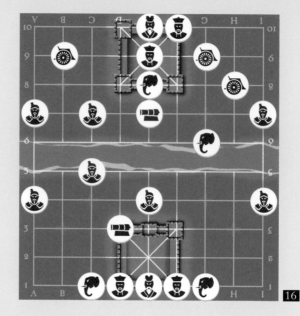

Block

Blocking the smooth movement of your foe's troops is a very important tactic, especially in setting up what is known as a smothered checkmate by blocking the progress of your opponent's Elephants. When using this tactic offensively, it's not enough simply to block the enemy pieces' movement with your own piece; instead, you want to force him to block himself with another of his troops, thus effectively neutralizing both of them. Blocking is therefore often used in conjunction with attracting, sacrificing one of your pieces in order to lure your enemy in between one of his other pieces and the spot you eventually want to occupy. Of course, you have to be careful that the piece you lure in does not threaten the point you want anyway!

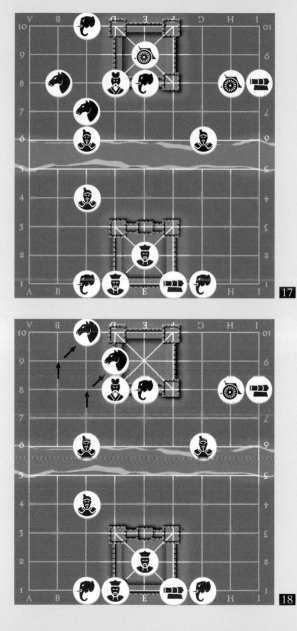

17

18

A typical example of blocking combined with attracting is shown in diagrams 17 and 18. In the initial position, the Blue Elephant has control over E8, an important point for attacking the King. Red moves a Chariot in between the Elephant and the desired point, forcing Blue to take the Chariot with his Horse. This means that the Horse now blocks the Elephant's eye, preventing it from capturing on E8, and that Red can now move a Horse to E8, checkmating.

Pin down

A useful tactic in any number of circumstances, offensive and defensive, this prevents an enemy piece from moving, because if it did so, the consequences would be disastrous. The best possible situation is one in which you pin down an enemy piece because if it were moved, the King would be placed in check, making the move illegal. Weaker forms of pinning down can be created in which the moving of the enemy piece would simply allow you to force a more powerful attack, but these are not anywhere near as effective as pinning down combined with check. Diagram 19 shows a typical pin down, where the Red Horse on E3 is prevented from moving, as doing so would result in the Blue Cannon on E6 checking Red's King.

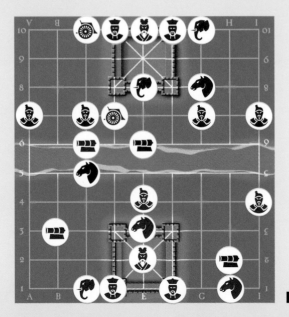

19

74

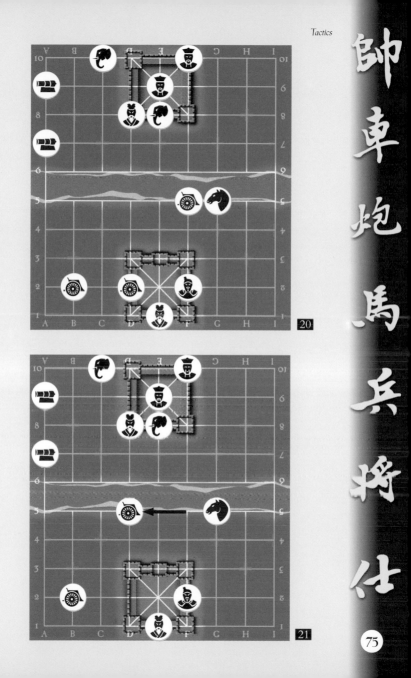

20

21

Freeing pieces

It is not unknown for a player to find that his own pieces are obstructing his movement. For example, diagram 20 shows a situation where the Red Chariot is blocking the Red Horse's leg, preventing it from moving to E6 where it could check the King. Simply moving the piece away is a bad move, as it loses you speed and allows your opponent to respond to the new threat posed by the freed piece. Instead, the moved piece should create a new threat of its own. In diagram 21, we can see that Red has moved the Chariot away to threaten the Blue Chariot. This ensures that Blue must capture the Red Chariot with the Blue Chariot on D2 (the position in diagram 21). Thus Red has drawn the Blue Chariot away from its previously threatening position, and freed the Horse to check the Blue King.

Retreating

Sometimes running away can be threatening in itself. When you retreat a piece in order to avoid capture, try to move it to a point where it either threatens a new attack or could do so within a move; do not simply move it to a 'safe' place. Diagram 22 shows a typical example, where the Blue Cannon has just retreated in order to avoid capture by the Red Cannon, but in doing so also threatens a smothered checkmate on Red. Red uses the same tactic next move, as we can see in diagram 23, retreating its Horse in order to protect the King.

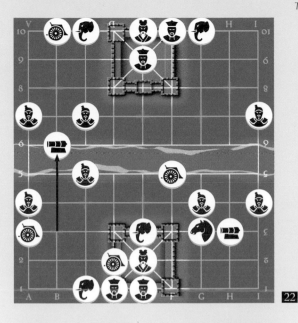

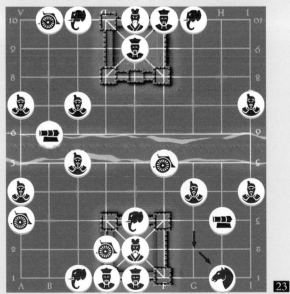

帥車炮馬兵將仕

Problems

These are all to play and mate, but they demonstrate some of the basic principles of good play.

Red to play and win in two.

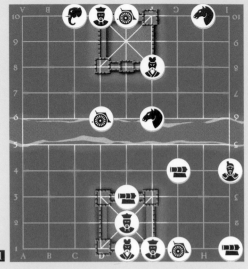

P1

P2

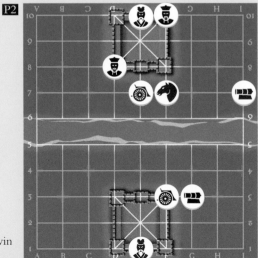

Red to play and win in four.

78

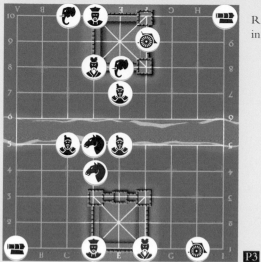

Red to play and win in four.

P3

P4

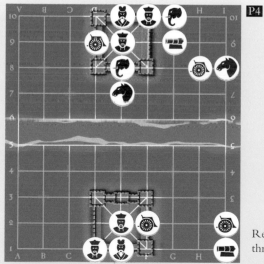

Red to play and win in three.

帥車炮馬兵將仕

79

相
車
砲
馬
卒
士
象

Solutions

A simple enough attack utilizing the unique properties of the Cannon.

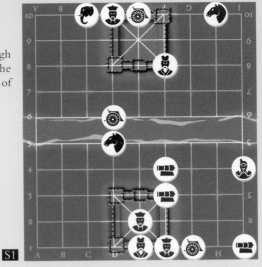

S1

S2

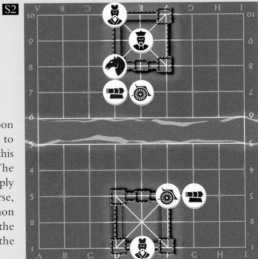

A very neat fork upon the two spaces next to the King finishes this sequence off. The Advisor cannot simply take the Horse, because the Cannon could still leap the Advisor, taking the King,

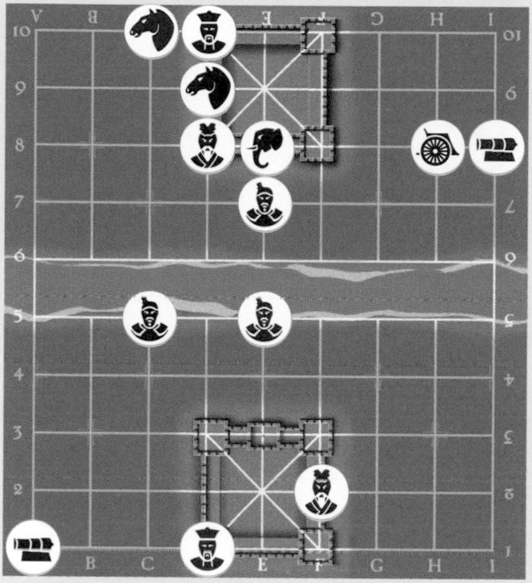

Firstly, the King is threatened by the Cannon, preventing the Blue Elephant from taking the Red Horse. The Red Chariot is then sacrificed to the Blue Horse, blocking the Elephant's eye and allowing a checkmate with the Red Horse.

S3

S4

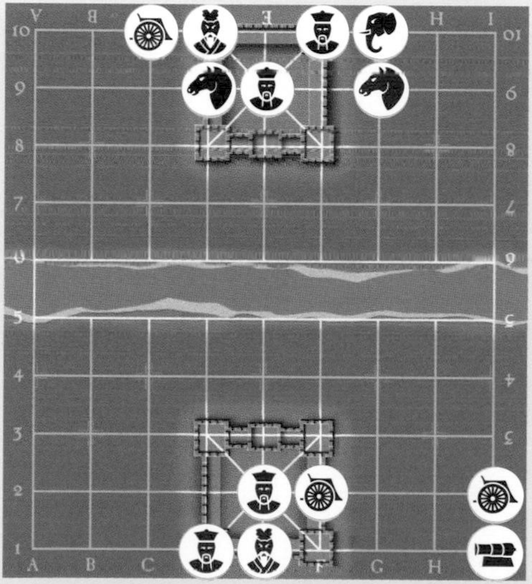

A beautiful example of clearing space; the Chariot and the Cannon are neatly sacrificed to create space for the Horse's attack.

帥車炮馬兵將仕

81

Endgame

The endgame is what everything comes down to. By now, there are very few pieces left and everything depends on the advantages gained in the previous stages of the game. To go through all the possible permutations of the endgame would be impossible, so I am merely going to cover some common scenarios and demonstrate some interesting checkmates. There are two basic rules that are especially important to the endgame.

Stalemate

Unlike in chess, stalemate in xiangqi results in the stalemated side losing. Remember that if, in xiangqi, you cannot move without putting yourself in check, you have lost. This is a vital part of many checkmates with a single piece. For instance, in diagram 1, the Blue King is unable to make a legitimate move, because moving to any of the positions next to him would put him in check to either the Pawn or the King. Making a loop move, where you repeat the same checking position three times or more, is also considered, in many circumstances, to be a stalemate, and results in the person who moves last losing the game.

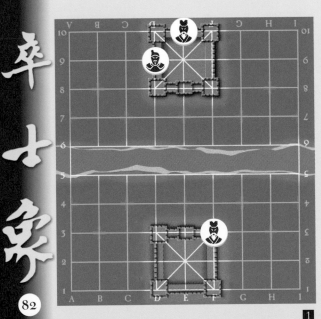

1

The key to winning using stalemates is to make waiting moves with your own King, in order to force your opponent to move next, such as simply advancing it backwards and forwards along the file.

It is possible to have a true draw in xiangqi – indeed, it is quite frequent. It only happens when both sides are equal and there is, according to theory, no true way to win the game. There are pages and pages of examples to determine this, and nobody really agrees too strongly on it. Unless you wish to be bogged down in argument, I suggest that you agree draws by simple mutual consent; it should be perfectly obvious when nobody is going to win.

The King Confrontation

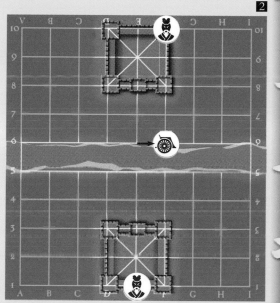

This rule is absolutely essential for checkmating. Remember, the two Kings cannot face each other across the board without any pieces in between. Making a move that would result in this situation is illegal. Essentially, think of Kings as having the ability to capture like Chariots, but only in order to take the other King.

Perhaps the most common checkmate uses a combination of this rule and a Chariot's power, driving the enemy King against the side of the Palace and pinning him between your King and the Chariot, as shown in diagram 2. All that is required for this very simple checkmate is checking the enemy King in the centre file, moving your own King to that file, defended by your Chariot, and then shifting your Chariot over to deliver the checkmate.

Be systematic

In the endgame, it is very easy to think many moves ahead, because the number of pieces involved is much fewer. You should be planning at least five moves or so ahead, because your opponent certainly will be! Ideally, you want to know exactly what is going to happen – what must happen – from your very first moves towards checkmate. This is not the time for spontaneity and bluff anymore, this is careful, systematic planning.

Piece and position

Every successful checkmate in the endgame (and not all do occur in the endgame, an unexpected checkmate is perfectly possible in the midgame, especially with less experienced players) comes down to the winning player coming into it with an advantage either in pieces or in positioning. Advantages in positioning are hard to explain, but the *Sample Game* contains an excellent example at the end.

Advantages in pieces are simpler to gauge. Coming out with a single extra Pawn can make all the difference. Come into the endgame a Chariot

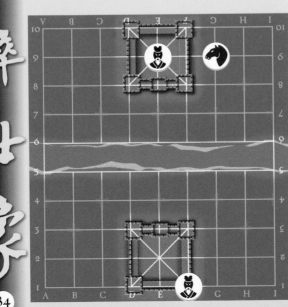

ahead, and your win is virtually guaranteed. In many endgames, the winner is quite obvious; the defender is merely trying to stall things and get him to make a stupid mistake. First of all, let us deal with some situations where one side has two pieces left, and the other only one. We have already shown you how to win with just a Chariot, so let us look at some other situations.

The lonesome Pawn

Obviously, it is impossible to checkmate if your only surviving pieces are defensive, such as Elephants, Advisors and Kings. It is perfectly possible, however, to win the game with just one Pawn and a King against your opponent's King. All you do is advance your Pawn over the River so that it gains the power to move sideways, then shift it over to either of the armpit files and gradually advance it, threatening the King where possible but always on his diagonal. If you cannot move the Pawn without the King being able to capture it, make a waiting move with your King instead. Eventually and inevitably, you should end up with the situation shown back in diagram 1.

Winning with a single Horse

If you only have one Horse left, it is still quite possible to checkmate a solitary King. Firstly, you have to drive away the King from the central file by threatening the spots above and below him, as shown in diagram 3. The King now must move, and must move to the sides. Once that is done, move your King onto the central file, so the enemy King is now pinned against the Palace walls by the King confrontation rule (as you will note, a common element of these strategies). Finally, threaten the points above and below the King again, as shown in diagram 4, and you will win a stalemate victory, with the enemy King unable to move.

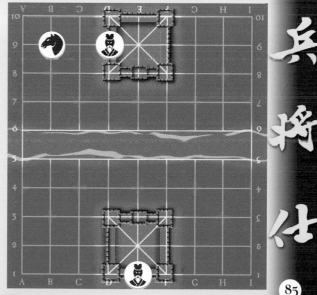

4

Winning with a single Cannon – and a little help

Clearly, a single Cannon on its own can never checkmate. Sure, it could use the King as a gun mount, but what difference would that make, given that Kings cannot confront anyway? So, to win with a Cannon, you also have to have a piece for it to jump. Advisors are normally good for this. If you have got the extra piece, the procedure is exactly the same as for the Horse; drive the enemy King away from the central file, move your King to the centre, and checkmate the pinned King with the Cannon and Advisor, or whatever other piece you are using. The only piece that cannot be used as a mount, unfortunately, is the ever-useless Elephant, because the only forward position in the Palace that in can occupy is in the central file.

Trickier situations

Unfortunately, it is actually fairly rare that a situation comes down to simply an advantage of one piece. Normally, there are a good many secondary pieces left, such as Advisors, Pawns, Elephants and suchlike, and things become more complicated. Here checkmate scenarios begin to concentrate on pinning the King between his own Advisors, or trapping him

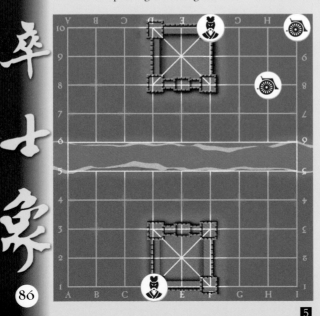

between the zones of control of two of your pieces. Often the critical element here can be simply who moves first at an important moment; there are often situations where the other side could have won if it was merely a move ahead, which only emphasises the importance of having the initiative throughout the game.

Double Chariot checkmates

If you are lucky or skilful enough to have come out of the midgame with both your Chariots, winning is a doddle. Simply force the unfortunate King further down or up with your Chariots, and eventually pin him against the bottom or top, skewered between one Chariot on the rank and one on the file, as shown in diagrams 5 to 7. With Blue to move in diagram 5, the only move possible is to F9, countered by Red moving a Chariot to H9 (diagram 6). The King is forced to F8 and mated by the Chariot moving to I8 (diagram 7). This holds true no matter what the opposition pieces are, provided one of your Chariots has a clear initial threat on the King and you are moving first.

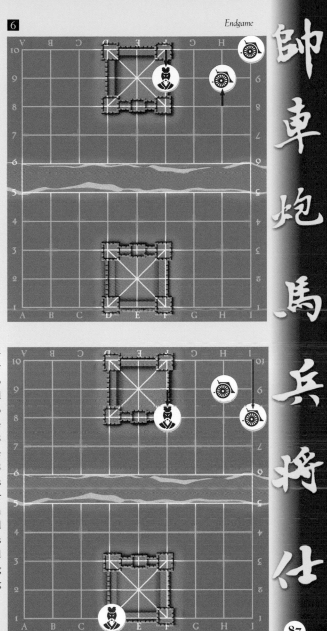

87

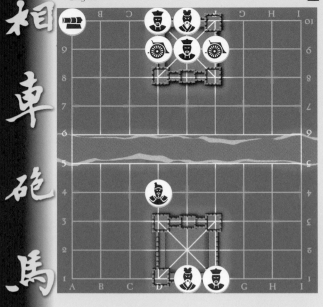

A trickier move, provided both your Chariots can get inside the Palace as in diagram 8, is to threaten your opponent's King with one up close. Here Blue has no choice but to retreat, as if he uses the Advisor to capture the threatening Chariot, he blocks his own passage and allows Red to move to the back rank and checkmate. Of course, the retreat also finishes in a checkmate, as diagram 9 shows - just a little later!

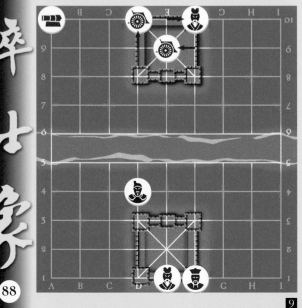

Double Cannon checkmates

Double Cannon are fairly easy to checkmate with, one using the other to jump over, and have the big advantage that the frontal piece can be taken and it is still checkmate, as the remaining Cannon can jump over the enemy piece that has just taken its companion. For instance, the situation shown in diagram 10 will soon result in checkmate, whatever happens. If Blue does nothing, Red's back Cannon happily takes its Chariot, and then has a checkmate on the King. However, if Blue takes the front Cannon, as in diagram 11, it's an immediate checkmate, as the back Cannon can now simply jump the Blue Chariot and capture the King - so this move would be illegal.

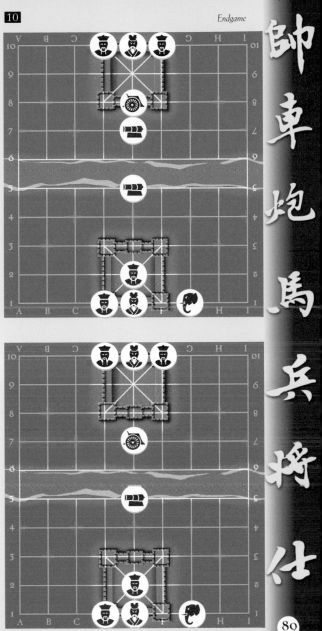

11

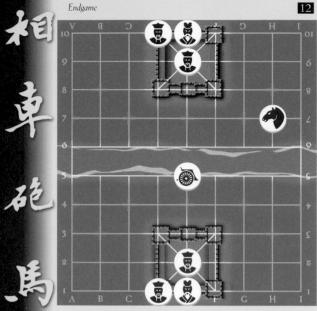

Elbowing Horse checkmate

A very common checkmate involves using a Horse and a Chariot or Cannon, as shown in diagrams 12 and 13. As you can see, it's terribly simple; firstly the Horse checks from the elbow file and forces the King to the Palace corner, and then the other offensive piece moves over for the checkmate.

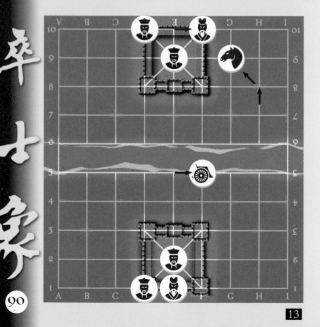

Horse from the corner checkmate

Slightly more complicated, this one. Firstly, you need to pin down your opponent's Advisor with a Chariot, as you can see in diagram 14. Once this is done, the Advisor is unable to move without putting the King illegally in check, and so cannot take the Horse when it moves into the Palace corner to check. The King is then forced over to the side, and the piece that was pinning it down can move over and checkmate, as demonstrated in diagram 15. A simpler version of this, lacking the original threat from the Advisor, is shown in diagrams 16 and 17. Here the Horse simply attacks, then the second piece moves in and checkmates. The King is unable to take the second piece, because the Horse has both positions forked.

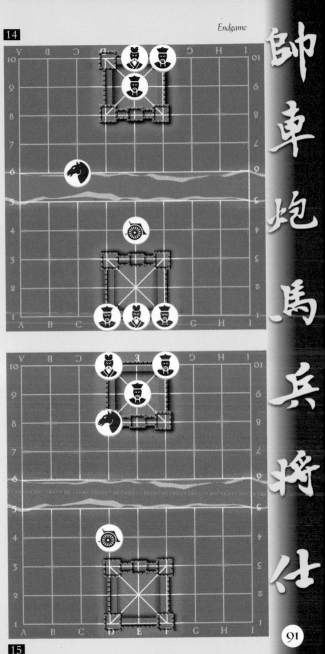

帥車炮馬兵將仕

91

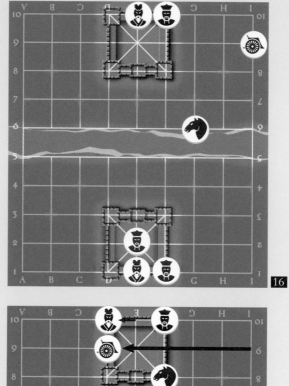

16

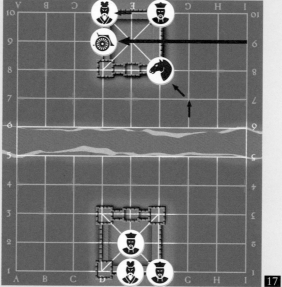

17

Angler Horse checkmate

Really, this is just another variation on the previous technique. The Horse threatens the King from the elbow file, forcing it inwards, as we can see in diagram 18. The Chariot then pulls up and checkmates it, as in diagram 19. I only put it in because one Chinese source describes the shape as 'like a chain of double elephants' and I would like anyone who can figure out what on earth that means to write to me and tell me!

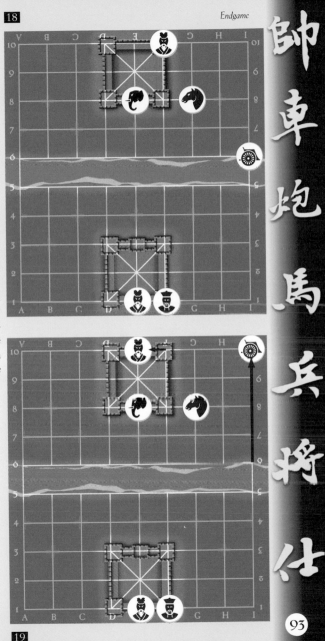

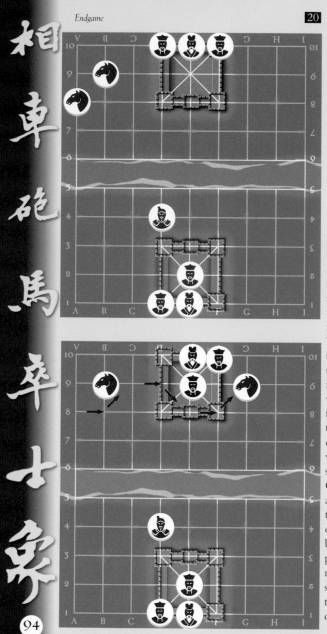

Rolling Horses checkmate

After all these Horse plus Chariot or Cannon examples, you are probably thinking, 'Sure, but what do I do if I've only got two Horses?' The answer is simple, as shown here. Firstly, bring both of them up on one side of the Palace, as seen in diagram 20. Then move the back one forwards, checking the King, which is forced to retreat. Roll it forward into the centre and check the King again, making it retreat back to where it began, then finally move over to the other side and checkmate. The whole process is shown in diagram 21. Of course, you can always try and bring the Horses up on either side from the beginning to try and pin the King in the middle, but this is less subtle and leaves them isolated and open to attack; best to start on one side and roll over.

Tiger silhouette checkmate

Great names are always a feature of xiangqi. This one is based on the idea of scaring prey away from its hiding place with the shadow of a tiger, allowing the real huntsmen to come in and trap it. In this case, the tiger is a Chariot, and the huntsman a Horse. This is a sharp, nasty checkmate, really best suited to the midgame, and can be pulled off if your opponent has foolishly exposed his King on one of the armpit files, as in diagram 22. Firstly, the Chariot moves up, checking the King and forcing it downwards. Then the Horse comes in, checking again. Forced downwards, the King is then pinned between the Chariot and the Horse and checkmated, as in diagram 23.

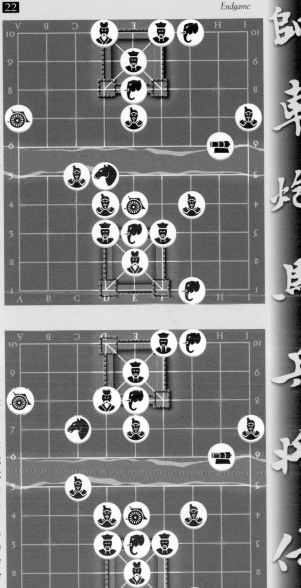

帥 車 炮 馬 兵 將 仕

Smothering Cannon checkmate

This checkmate exploits the useful property of Cannon to jump enemy pieces that have just captured their friends, eventually smothering the enemy King within his own pieces. Diagrams 24 and 25 show the procedure. The first Cannon takes the Blue Elephant and is then taken by the Chariot, which is taken in turn by the second Cannon, also dlivering a final checkmate to the King.

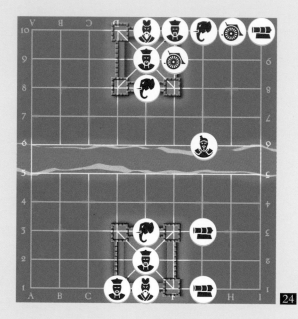

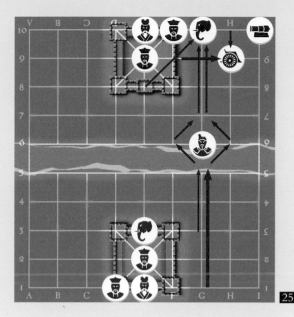

25

Three Chariots checkmate

So-called because a Pawn inside the enemy Palace is said to have nearly the power of a Chariot, and combining it with two other Chariots – sometimes possible in the midgame – produces a deadly force. Diagram 26 shows a typical checkmate about to be achieved through this combined force.

Two ghosts knocking on the door checkmate

A beautiful little checkmate using two Pawns and the power of a King confrontation, and again demonstrating their vicious offensive power within the walls of the Palace. Once they are near the King, as shown in diagram 27, there is very little that can be done to stop them, as diagram 28 shows. Melodramatic players may want to rap on the table as they threaten this sequence of moves.

相
車
砲
馬
卒
士
象

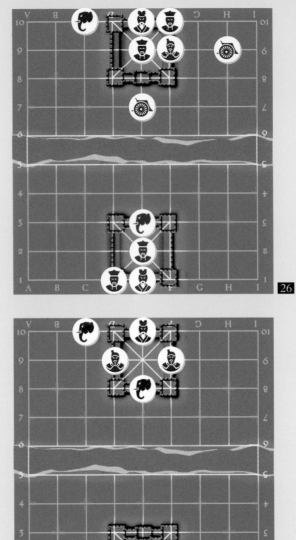

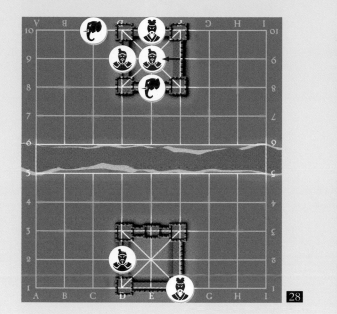

28

Throat cutting checkmate

This combination of Chariots and Cannons close-up is a nasty set of moves. Firstly, one Chariot moves into the Palace, supported by the Cannon just outside, as seen in diagram 29. It then repeatedly checks the King, eventually forcing it to retreat into a central position where the second Chariot can deliver a checkmate, finally bringing the second Chariot up in support and forcing the King into the corner for a checkmate, as we see in diagram 30.

And finally – the three piece checkmate

You would have though that checkmating with three pieces would be easy – and it is, fairly. Virtually nothing can stop a combination of three pieces, especially concentrated on one side as in diagram 31. Two of them combine to check repeatedly the King, and then finally the Cannon is brought up to deliver the killing blow, as shown in diagram 32.

帥車炮馬兵將仕

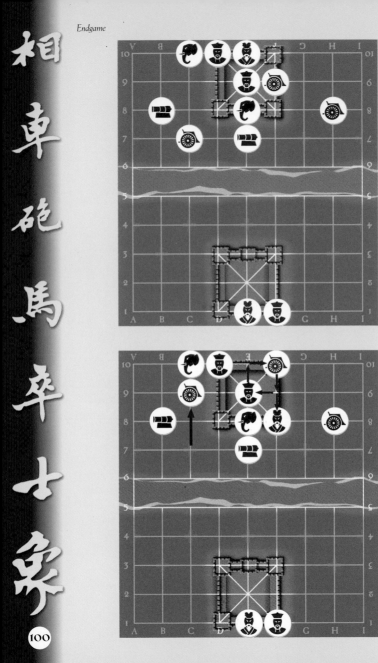

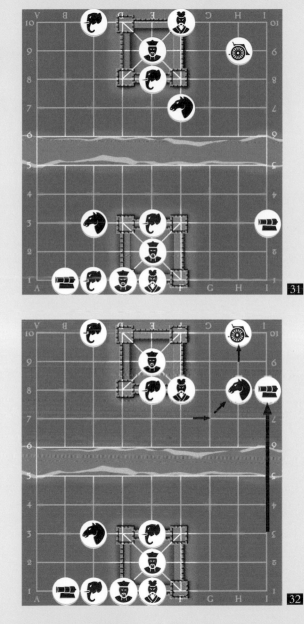

31

32

帥 車 炮 馬 兵 將 仕

Dirty Tricks

The most violent time in Chinese history was perhaps that of the Warring States, where several early kingdoms fought a series of bloody and brutal wars to determine who would have control over the territory that is now China. The successful generals of that period had one strong factor in common – they fought dirty. Boobytraps, straw men to make your numbers bigger, gradually reducing the number of fires you lit at night to make your opponent think your men were deserting, bribing your opponent's troops, making sure you had a spy in his tent, watching his every move – nothing was too low for a good general. It was also during this period that xiangqi was developed, and the mentality of the time informs the tactics of the game.

The notions of honour or chivalry are largely foreign to the Chinese conception of war, which is brutally pragmatic; you are in it to win. What is the point in fighting if you do not use every means possible? Anything else is a betrayal of yourself and your men. If you want to be a successful xiangqi player, not at an abstract but at a practical level, you might do well to adopt the same attitude. Remember, you are not playing for the love of the game, or for a chivalrous competition, you are playing flat-out to win, and you should do anything to get there. It may not be a nice attitude, but it is an effective one.

This chapter is chock-full of mean things to do when playing xiangqi; how to psych out your opponent, exploit his weaknesses, and distract him from his strategy. You probably should not use them when playing your little sister, and some of them are just plain unsporting and best used on good friends, but several of them are applicable to just about any game. It is also useful to know the tricks that can be pulled, so that you can learn to counter them if, for some strange reason, you are planning on playing fair yourself.

Your enemy is an ignorant western barbarian

Your first games of xiangqi may well be with people who are far more used to playing chess. If they are much better at chess than you, this is a good opportunity to beat them solid. They may know all the rules, but certain habits tend to carry over from one game into another, and you can exploit these. Think of yourself as an intelligent and cultured Chinese general crushing the stupid and brutal foreigner, and you cannot go far wrong.

Firstly, chess players are given to playing much more aggressively in the opening game than is wise in xiangqi. They tend to send their Chariots and Cannon forward as soon as possible, often without giving them adequate support. As well as being likely to result in the capture of the attacking piece, this will leave a fatal hole in their defences, as discussed in *Opening the Game*. Be prepared for this, and ready to make a counterattack that exploits their weakness.

Chess players are also liable to fall victim to preconceptions about how the pieces move. If you move fast and subtly enough, your opponent may make moves based upon the assumption, for instance, that Pawns capture diagonally, or that Horses can jump. Chess players often forget the limitations of the Palace. Force your opponent's pieces over to the side of the Palace, and he may well forget that he cannot move them further and be pinned down in checkmate. The King Confrontation rule is another valuable tool here, as chess lacks anything remotely resembling this rule.

Know your enemy

It is always important to remember that you are not playing some abstract opponent, you are playing a real person. Learn to read your opponent's body language. Watch where on the board he looks at, which pieces his fingers stray near before finally moving. Play your own fingers over the board before moving, and watch for the pieces he twitches when you go near. Often, after moving, a player becomes aware of a fatal weakness he has just created and spends his time praying his opponent will not notice it; try and work out what these are. Go over any other games you have played against him. Does he particularly favour certain pieces? A lot of players overuse the attacking troops; is he prone to that? How did you checkmate him last time? He will be watching out for that this time, and you can use the threat of it to distract him from the real danger.

At the same time as you try to read your opponent's mind, you should be giving out disinformation yourself. Do not try to keep a poker face; that is never convincing, because your true intentions will always slip through in little signals. Silly facial expressions of dissatisfaction fool nobody. Learn to lie with your eyes. If you are a really good player, you can work over the board in your mind and a casual glance should suffice to check position; you do not need to stare at particular area – but you can do it in order to fool your opponent. Become aware of your own body language when playing and try and adopt unfamiliar habits. If you clench your hand when you are nervous, do it when you are not and watch him try to find a weakness where there is none. If you can deceive him into thinking you are planning something you are not, you are halfway towards winning the game already.

Some players assume a totally different persona when playing, becoming cold calculating machines or wild lunatics; this throws your opponent, until he begins to get used to that persona. Start shifting persona; experiment with new play styles, try and develop new habits and break old ones – anything that stops your opponent successfully analysing your plans.

Half the battle is in the mind

A good part of real xiangqi play is your state of mind; you have to care about winning, but not become so passionate about it that you become distracted from the game in hand. The best players generally have an attitude of cool detachment towards a game, combined with a steely determination to win. Different Grand Masters have different approaches; some are noted for regarding the board with a calm, regal eye, others curse under their breath and appear to be about to explode.

To be in the best state of mind to play xiangqi, you have to remember two things. Firstly, it is only a game, and secondly, it is more important than anything else in the world! Maintaining a balance between those two positions is vital; you cannot achieve the necessary detachment required to analyse your situation properly without the first, and you cannot pull off the unexpected and desperate strokes of brilliance without the second.

At the same time, you want to prevent your opponent from achieving this state of mind; forcing him to become so involved in the details of the game that he loses sight of the overall picture of things. The idea is to worry him, in both senses of the word, so that he is always concerned with immediate defensive measures and does not have the chance to plan his own attacks.

For instance, there are often weaknesses in a player's defence that are not actually weaknesses at all, but will resolve themselves after a few moves – perhaps even strengthening that player's position after the situation has been played out. Nonetheless, it can be worth targeting these, because it temporarily focuses your opponent's attention on them, distracting him from other possible manoeuvres and forcing him onto the defensive. If you have him sufficiently worried, he may even make a poor move as a consequence, creating a weakness where there was none before.

Different players have different approaches to disconcerting their opponent. Some like to keep up a constant barrier of questions ('Hmm. Interesting move. Are you quite certain? I'll let you take it back if you want?'), others prefer an icy silence. The way you move your own pieces can be important; if you are trying to worry your opponent, than whatever move you make, do it decisively, as though it exposes a fatal weakness in his troops. Stamp the piece down on the board firmly, or perhaps twist it around in your fingers as you place it as though operating a corkscrew – an unexpectedly distracting move. Think playground tactics here, though I would not stoop quite as low as whistling.

Feinting

As I have stated umpteen times, it is vital when playing xiangqi to be working towards a definite goal at all times. Just moving for the sake of it is pointless; you have to be acting to achieve a certain objective. Almost as vital, however, is keeping your opponent from working out what this objective is. This is where feinting comes in.

The idea of feinting comes originally from fencing, where a feint is a quick faked strike intended to distract the fencer's opponent from where the strike will really land. In xiangqi, it has much the same purpose; it fools your opponent into thinking that your offensive will be aimed other than where you really intend to attack.

To be convincing, a feint must look as though it could really lead to an attack. The best time to feint is when you can see two equally appealing options for attack. If you appear to be aiming for one, your opponent will begin the procedure of defending against that, and hopefully not notice the threat elsewhere. Of course, if your foe appears to be insufficiently prepared against your feigned attack, carry on with it as if it were real all along!

A riskier type of threat is the move that seems to be useless – because it is. For instance, sending an unprotected Chariot into enemy territory, or randomly leaping a Horse out in front. This can be a good, if dangerous move when you are all out of ideas for the moment, or if your opponent seems to be about to launch a strong attack. The point of this is to confuse your opponent; make him think that you have got some cunning plan that he cannot see. If you fool him successfully, he will probably assume an extremely defensive position, buying you sufficient time to think up a real plan. Alternatively, a far-flung feint like this can be a simple sacrifice move, throwing away the feinting piece to distract your opponent's attention from the flank you are really attacking on.

Responding to the first type of feint is difficult; after all, the whole point is that it could be a convincing attack. Try to respond using pieces already concentrated on one side of the board, rather than shifting pieces in from elsewhere and leaving possible weaknesses. The second type of feint is easier to respond to, as long as you have confidence in yourself and can remember that if you do not know what your opponent is doing, he might not either! Either cut off and kill the feinting piece or riposte by using the weakness he has just created by shifting a piece forwards to thrust into the gap left.

Trapping

Traps are, in a way, the opposite of feints. A feint is a distracting offensive move; a trap is a defensive set-up that seems vulnerable and encourages your opponent to attack, but which will in fact result in the defender having the advantage.

The basic type of trap exploits people's tendencies to forget about the abilities of certain pieces. Setting up situations where your opponent can check you by moving right next to your King is a typical example of this; many inexperienced players (and the occasional absent-minded experienced player) will instinctively seize the opportunity, and then kick themselves as you smugly take the piece with the King. Much the same trick can be pulled off with the Advisors. Of course, make sure that the attack comes within the walls of the Palace, or you may well have just inadvertently checkmated yourself. Similarly, attackers often forget about Elephants, especially if you keep them in their starting positions. A nasty little trap can be created by keeping your Elephants back and encouraging your foe to move onto E3 or E8, as appropriate.

The Cannon is a superb trapping piece. This may not seem like its most obvious use, but it is true. A Cannon can sit in your territory, surrounded by other pieces, and happily control both a rank and file. When most people check whether somewhere they want to move to is defended, too, they often instinctively look only at those pieces that have straight lines to the spot, and neglect the Cannon.

More cunning traps involve luring an enemy piece forward with a tantalizing opening. If your enemy has any sense, he will attack with a supported piece. Rather than attacking the supported piece, then, you attack the piece that is providing the support. Once that piece is removed – whether by capture or retreat – you can then proceed neatly to take the original attacker. This is a variant of the strategy of attraction described in *Tactics*.

Sometimes, you may spot a weakness in your own defences that cannot be easily corrected in one move, and which your opponent has not spotted. In this case, you might voluntarily create a weakness elsewhere, distracting your foe from spotting the real weakness, and giving you time to solve the real problem.

Playing nice

However tempting trickery and deceit are, remember that etiquette is a big part of Chinese culture. Nothing excuses rudeness, especially about a game. Being polite is vital, especially if you want to play that opponent again. If he asks you to stop a particular twitch or habit, then do so. When a game is clearly a draw, admit it rather than trying to force a victory; it will save both of you time.

This holds twice as true when playing on-line. Remember that xiangqi players are a fairly close-knit community, even electronically, and that bad behaviour will soon become known. Some on-line programs have fairly easily exploitable quirks that will allow you to cheat and win a game unfairly, raising your rankings, but it will soon become known that you are doing this and you will be ostracized – and possibly even banned from a site. Due to the distances involved in on-line play, it is also often tempting to be rude to your opponent; do not. Never say anything over e-mail that you would not say to somebody's face.

Sample Game

Hu Rong Hua is one of the great modern xiangqi players and holds the status of International Grandmaster. Born in 1945, he was a child prodigy, and soon found himself being trained by some of the best players in China at the Shanghai Academy. He stunned the xiangqi world when, at the age of only fifteen, he won both the Hangzhou Five-Province Tournament and the keenly contested Fifth National Open Tournament which he recently won again at the age of fifty-two!

This game sees Hu, playing Blue, taking on Grandmaster Yang Guan Lin, known as the 'Chess Devil' in the National Open Tournament of 1960. A marvellous, hard-fought game, it begins with a series of swift attacks but has a long midgame and endgame. Both sides demonstrate good play at all three stages of the game, but Hu is generally on the offensive, and Yang the defensive. At a certain point in the game, it becomes obvious that Hu will win unless he makes a serious mistake, but Yang continues to play on, hoping to force him into an error, a typical sign of the determination it takes to make a Grandmaster.

Hu Rong
Hua

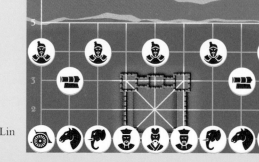

Yang
Guan Lin

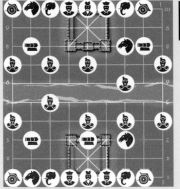

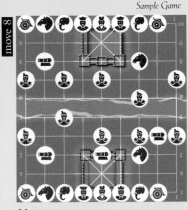

Moves 1 to 7: This is a pretty standard open‐ing on both sides, so far. Yang has taken the tra‐ditional approach of a central attack, while Hu is clearly concentrating his forces on his right. Yang has wisely taken the precaution of freeing his right-hand Chariot in order to defend against a foreseen attack from Hu, and both sides have tentatively advanced their Pawns.

Move 8: It can be argued that this early attack is really the deciding point in the game! This pre‐viously rarely seen attack was the product of detailed research and analysis in the xiangqi acad‐emy at Shanghai, and has been shown to be one of the most devastating of initial openings. Now‐adays, savvy players counter it by moving their Chariot forward from H1 (or B1, if the attack is on the left) to their opponent's river bank.

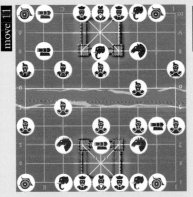

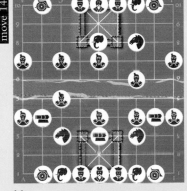

Moves 9 to 11: Yang counterattacks on the left, taking a Horse. Clearly, he is going to lose his Cannon to Hu's Chariot next move, but this is in fact part of his plan – a classic example of attracting a foe's piece to a bad position. Normally, exchanging a Cannon for a Horse would be a bad idea, but here it results in Hu's Chariot being blocked by the Cannon in front of it, restricting its movement and meaning Yang gains an edge in impetus.

Moves 12 to 14: Hu's first move, naturally, is to take the Cannon. Yang shifts over a Chariot to guard the second file, and Hu then responds by shifting his own Cannon into position. He now has two Cannon in Yang's territory; a very strong offensive combination. Hu is definitely setting up a strong offensive here, which, as we will see, will prove psychologically as well as purely tactically effective.

相
車
砲
馬
卒
士
象

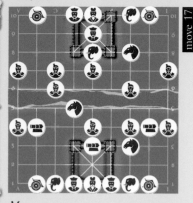

move 17

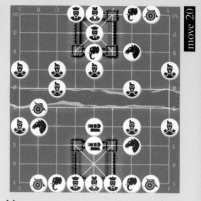

move 20

Moves 15 to 17: Keen to take Hu's Cannon, Yang proves overly greedy. Moving the Horse into position to take the Cannon gives Hu an advantage in impetus that he will press keenly throughout the rest of the game, including time to get his Advisor into a more defensive position.

Moves 18 to 20: Yang is now a Cannon ahead, but has handed the initiative decidedly over to Hu, who proceeds to press his attack fiercely, forcing a central check on Yang with his other Cannon. This is an excellent example of how it can often be worth abandoning a piece in order to gain an advantage in speed.

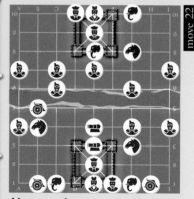

move 22

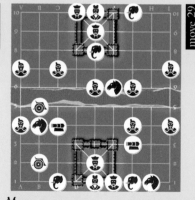

move 29

Moves 21 and 22: Yang is forced to counter Hu's check. Hu then captures Yang's Chariot with his own, which will force Yang to take it in return, removing the threat from the Horse on G3 to Hu's Cannon. Notice how Hu knows what pieces he wants to make the basis of his attack, and is not afraid to sacrifice or exchange pieces he is not planning to use in order to keep the attacking pieces safe.

Moves 23 to 29: After the initial wave of attack and response, both sides play cautiously for a little while, gradually shifting their positions. In particular, Hu brings his Horse forward to support his attacking Cannon, which has been criticized as an overly cautious move that allows Yang to recover some positional advantage. Pawn movements are common in this type of play, and we can see that both Yang and Hu have advanced their Pawns somewhat in lieu of more aggressive actions, each unwilling to force play into a more decisive mode.

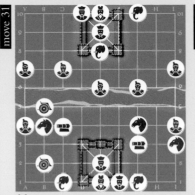

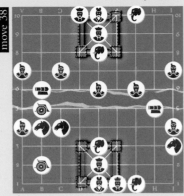

Moves 30 to 32: Hu takes Yang's Pawn with his Horse, and Yang responds by threatening Hu's Horse with his own. Hu has to retreat, but has come out of this encounter distinctly ahead; he has taken a Pawn, his Horse has moved to a better, more central position, and Yang's Horse has been pushed into the relatively useless edge file. When making this kind of short raid on a particular piece, remember that it is often better to retreat to a different position than the one you were originally in.

Moves 33 to 38: A series of gradual moves eventually sets up an intricate threat-counter-threat situation in the bottom left, where several powerful pieces – Horses, Cannons, and Chariots – are now locked together. The players are unwilling to make the first move in a sequence that will inevitably end in the capture of strong pieces on both sides.

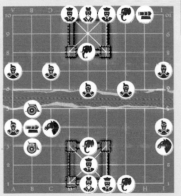

Moves 39 to 42: Yang makes an impetuous and somewhat foolish check on Hu, which he smoothly counters with his Advisor. Yang then realizes that he is now doomed to lose a piece in the bottom left, and moves the Chariot forward to ensure it is not taken by Hu's Horse, leaving Hu to take Yang's Horse instead.

Moves 43 and 44: Yang attempts to lure Hu's Cannon out with the tempting prospect of his Horse, but Hu does not fall into the trap. If he had done, his pieces would have become separated, Yang could take his Chariot, and he would lose the advantage. Instead, he moves his Pawn forward in a sacrificial move, threatening Yang's Horse in a new way and ensuring that Yang's Elephant is lured well away from the left-hand side where Hu's pieces are currently based.

相
車
砲
馬
卒
士
象

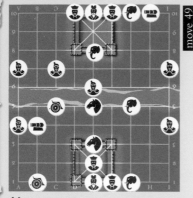

move 49

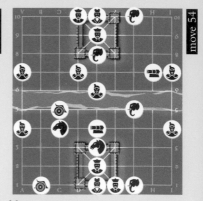

move 54

Moves 45 to 49: Hu threatens Yang's Horse, forcing another retreat and meaning that Yang's troops are now dangerously clustered within the Palace. Yang's retreat with his Chariot, rather than taking Hu's Cannon, may seem odd at first, but unless Yang protects the back row, Hu can make a very easy smothered checkmate with his own Chariot.

Moves 50 to 54: Moving his Cannon into the centre file again, Hu makes a rare mistake, weakening his attack by being overeager. Instead, he should have taken Yang's Pawn in his territory, in which case he could have slowly advanced his Pawns and trapped Yang from all sides. Yang pulls his Cannon back to threaten a check from the centre file, prevented by Hu's pre-emptive moving of his Advisor.

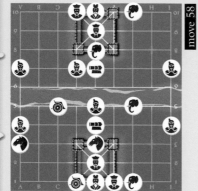

move 58

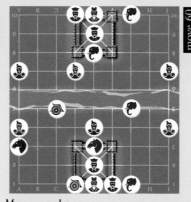

move 60

Moves 55 to 58: Yang makes a strong attack in the centre file, threatening Hu's Cannon, which has been the mainstay of his attack so far. Hu responds by threatening Yang's Chariot, forcing it away from its previously threatening position and into an already dangerously crowded Palace. In order to support his Cannon, Hu then advances his Pawn, ensuring that Yang's threatened capture will result in the loss of his own Cannon.

Moves 59 and 60: Yang forces the threatened exchange. It is difficult to say who has come out ahead after this. Hu's Pawn is now in a position to attack the Red Palace, but the Cannon also seems to have been crucial to his original battle plan. Yang's targeting of it was therefore very sensible; Hu's recovery from this loss, though, shows the flexibility of the best players.

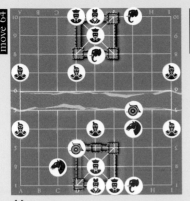

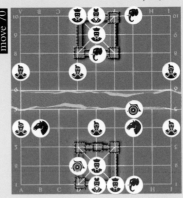

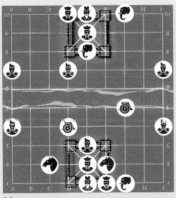

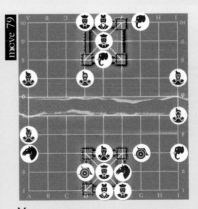

Moves 61 to 64: A typical sequence of threats, a good example of later midgame play, and also of the way that Hu has Yang's pieces pinned around the Palace. At first, Yang moves his Horse away from where the Pawn threatens it. He only has one choice of where to move, because Hu's Horse controls the other two possible squares. Hu brings his Chariot over to threaten Yang's Horse again, conveniently removing the Elephant in the process. In a good example of the value of a counterattack, Yang threatens Hu's Horse in return, rather than sim-

ply retreating his Horse, which would leave the initiative completely in Hu's hands. Hu does the same, moving his Horse out of danger's way, but also checking Yang's King at the same time.

Moves 65 to 70: Yang blocks Hu's check and threatens his Horse. It retreats, prompting a series of fairly futile moves that exactly repeat the previous positions (an exact duplication of moves 62 to 65). In order to end this, Hu retreats to a different spot.

Moves 71 to 74: After all that, Yang is forced simply to have his Horse retreat anyway! Hu takes advantage of the crowded nature of Yang's Palace, and begins to close in, moving his Pawn into a very threatening position and, in response to Yang's threat with his Chariot, checking the Red King with his Horse.

Moves 75 to 79: Yang blocks the check with his Chariot yet again, then threatens Hu's Chariot with his Elephant. Hu simply moves it in closer, putting Yang's pieces in even more of a clinch.

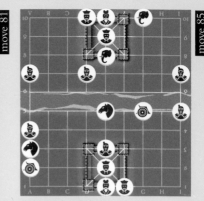

Moves 80 and 81: Although it may not seem so at first, Yang's moving his Horse forward here is an extremely clever move, as we will shortly see, although it results in the sacrifice of his Elephant. Both sides, as normal, have been somewhat profligate with their Elephants,

which are, after all, fairly useless pieces.

Moves 82 to 85: Yang forces Hu's Chariot to chase his Horse, and sets up his own Chariot to take the Blue Horse in return.

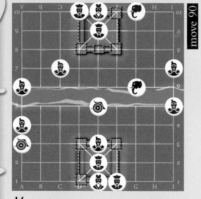

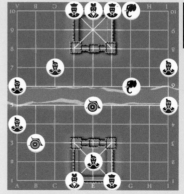

Moves 86 to 90: The exchange of Horses shown here is what Yang has been working towards since move 80. This is good play. Although it results in an equal loss for both sides, Yang already knows that he has probably lost, and his best chance is to stretch out the game, pick pieces off, and hope for a draw or for the young Hu to make a bad mistake. Exchanging Horses, therefore, hurts Hu much more than it does Yang. A little manoeuvring then goes on in Blue territory, and Hu advances his Pawn.

Moves 91 to 94: By now, the game has really entered its last stages, although in terms of moves played it is only a little more than half-way through. There is only one serious offensive piece left on either side – the Chariots – and it is Hu's advantage in Pawns and positioning that gives him his advantage. Here, Hu moves his Advisor to threaten a later King Confrontation. Yang shifts his own King as a result, allowing Hu to advance his Pawn further, removing a Red Advisor. The absence of this Advisor will be essential to Hu's final checkmate.

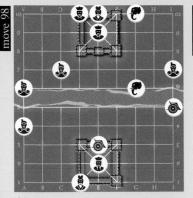

Moves 95 to 98: Here, Hu wisely does not risk his Chariot in an attack, as doing so would likely result in its capture. Instead, he begins to pick off the Red Pawns. Yang makes a desultory checkmate, which is easily blocked with the Advisor.

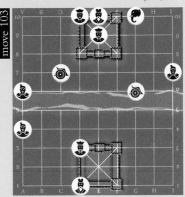

Moves 99 to 103: Hu continues to remove Yang's Pawns, ignoring the loss of his Elephant. Well and truly into the endgame now, the rest of play will consist of the manoeuvres of the two Chariots.

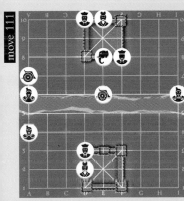

Moves 104 to 111: Frankly, this is pretty much just posturing. Yang is attempting to drag out the game for as long as possible, and these moves are fairly insignificant.

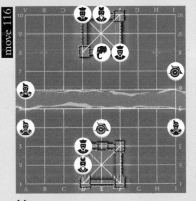

Moves 112 to 116: A good example of a Pawn chase. Yang constantly threatens Hu's Pawn, which continues to advance, hoping to force it to the back row, where it can then be taken. Hu ends this sequence by bringing his Chariot over in support of the Pawn.

帥車炮馬兵將仕

相車砲馬卒士象

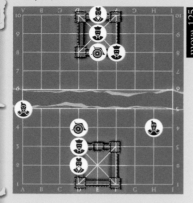

move 125

Moves 117 to 125: Here, we can see that Hu has blithely sacrificed his Pawn and an Elephant in order to buy time to shift his King and Chariot into the perfect set-up for an eventual checkmate using a King Confrontation.

move 130

Moves 126 to 130: Hu brings his Pawn over from the right-hand side to threaten the Red Palace again, and then uses his Chariot to threaten the Pawn that Yang has been gradually advancing forward on the left. A Pawn chase is inevitable here.

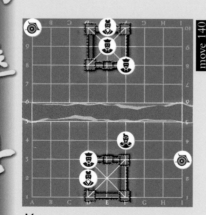

move 140

Moves 131 to 140: A long Pawn chase up the left-hand side of the board, ending, as has been obvious all along, with the capture of the Pawn when it reaches the corner. Really, Yang is just trying to save face at this point by stretching the game out further.

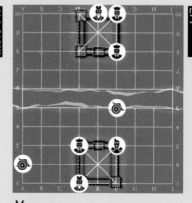

move 147

Moves 141 to 156: A final sequence of manoeuvres ends in Hu setting up the combination of Chariot and King Confrontation he has been planning since the start of the endgame. His advantage in Pawns and the earlier loss of Yang's Advisor made this pretty much a foregone conclusion. At this point, Yang finally surrenders, as checkmate is now inevitable.

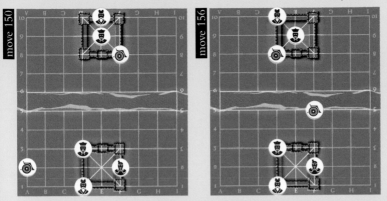

Why is it inevitable? Well, whatever Yang does next (probably taking the Blue Pawn), Hu takes his Advisor, and checks his King. Left with only a King and a Chariot against a King, Advisor, and Chariot, Yang realizes that he must lose, pinned between the Chariot and the King Confrontation, and so he surrenders.

Evaluating the game

What lessons can this fine game teach a xiangqi player? Firstly, Hu's initial attack is a very lovely opening, for which his opponent was not prepared. Strong, vicious, and unexpected, it meant that this part of the game was very short. The game shows the varying speeds of xiangqi. At several points play speeds up considerably, such as moves 14 to 22, and at others, like 23 to 29, or the long pawn chases at the end, slows down. Knowing when to force the speed of a game up, and when to let your opponent make the first move, is a vital skill.

As for the players, well, on Yang's part, he fought the game to the bitter end – dull, but worthy. He was also a fine judge of when an exchange of pieces would lead to an advantage. He knew for instance, that losing the Cannon and the Horse in the late midgame hurt Hu much more than himself.

Most noticeably, Hu had a strong offensive plan, making good use of his Cannon from the beginning, and stuck to it, willingly sacrificing pieces that were not involved. Not only that, he was willing to change his plan when necessity dictated, showing himself to be a fine adaptive player. Of course, his play was flawed on a number of occasions, chiefly through becoming a little too obsessed about defending his central Cannon, which caused the tempo of his play to be slower than it should have been. Still, his offence, from the beginning, was strong enough to give him a crucial advantage in the end game. Whenever Yang tried to block or threaten his pieces, he always attacked rather than retreated, meaning that most significant play took place in the Red Territory.

Cultural Background

Without doubt, xiangqi is one of the oldest board games in the world. Arguably, it is the oldest form of chess, although this is, to say the least, hotly disputed. Most histories of chess claim that the game was invented in India in the 6th century AD, and that xiangqi was then brought from India to China, perhaps via the silk trade routes.

On the other hand, there seem to be references to xiangqi in very early Chinese literature, right back to the Warring States period of 480 to 221 BC, where several kingdoms struggled in a series of vicious battles that eventually resulted in the triumph of the Qin and the establishment of China. It makes sense that a game so based on battle might emerge out of a period like this, and the pieces represent the major troop types of the time especially, of course, the Chariots, which died out of warfare soon afterwards.

Chess historians have often confused this earlier game with wei-chi or Go, the oldest board game in the world. From the surviving descriptions, however, it appears to be much closer to xiangqi. This raises the interesting possibility that chess really came from China to India and from India, of course, to the West. Xiangqi, therefore, could well be the original form of chess.

Western chess historians, for whom this seems to be something of a personal insult, often claim that xiangqi is in fact a separately evolved game, pointing to the river, the palaces, and so forth. It seems obvious, however, if you do not have an agenda to promote, that the two games, compared to other board games, have far too much in common to account for by any means other than a historical link. Early versions of Indian chess, too, have even more features in common, such as the two-square diagonal move and the Advisor piece; the Bishop and Queen that we are used to were added in Europe around the end of the 15th century.

The name xiangqi itself is much argued over. Literally, it means the elephant game, which has often been argued as pointing to an Indian origin. Elephants are, obviously, a big part of Indian culture, and the Western bishop is an elephant in Indian chess – and, indeed, is still referred to as an elephant in Russian and Spanish. However, elephants do seem to have existed in China, as there are plenty of references to them in legend, and to have been used in ancient warfare.

Some Chinese scholars argue, too, that the word xiang originally had a different meaning. For instance, when xiang is linked with another character, its meaning changes to being a constellation of stars, and so the game might conceivably stem from astrology, and have, just conceivably, been used in divination. (Another fact to impress people with: the system of Chinese characters itself seems to have evolved out of divining by heating and cracking tortoise shells, and then reading the lines.) The relative weakness of the elephant within xiangqi, which is odd considering the strength and offensive force of elephants in ancient warfare, also suggests a linguistic confusion somewhere along the way.

Most Chinese people will be very pleased if you support the view that chess started in China; like the British, they like to think they invented everything! It is not, as I say, a popular view in Western and Indian circles, however, though it is becoming more commonly accepted.

Evolution

Xiangqi seems to have taken on a pretty definite form by around the 9th century; it's rather hard to tell before that. There certainly appear to be lots of references to the game, but it may well have had a very different form. In 568 AD, Emperor Wu collected information on and made improvements to a game called xiangxi, but unfortunately, the only surviving articles are rather scholarly ones, and it's hard to tell how the game was played. The pieces seem to have been more cosmic in nature, including dragons, suns, stars, and such like, which supports the astrological argument mentioned earlier.

One source reports that the sun, moon, and stars were replaced with Horses, Chariots, and Pawns in 839 AD, which might be taken as the start of real xiangqi. However, some stories seem to have these pieces being used earlier – but these could be made up later, of course.

Wherever it started, early xiangqi was certainly somewhat different to the modern version. To begin with, there was no Cannon, which seems to have been added sometime in the 10th century AD, and does not exist in similar games such as Korean chess. The River, too, is probably a later addition, designed simply to mark off the two sides' territories. It is often known as the Yellow River, one of the major Chinese waterways and an important feature in some of the battles of the warring states. The board may have originally been bigger – nobody's really certain – and it is possible that pieces may originally have been placed on the squares rather than the points. Playing on points might well have been borrowed from another popular Chinese game, wei-chi/go.

Two myths

One of xiangqi's popular nicknames, Happiness Inside an Orange, comes from a legend of the Tang dynasty, recorded in a book called Xuan Qui Lu. It tells of a family in Sichuan province who had a strange mandarin tree in their garden, with two very oddly shaped, huge mandarins on it. When broken in half, each of the mandarins turned out to contain two little old men playing xiangxi! What was done with the little old men, the story doesn't record; presumably they were left to keep on happily playing.

Another interesting story from Xuan Qui Lu is recorded as happening in 762 AD, and refers very clearly to the rules of xiangqi as we know them. There was a poor man called Cen Shun who lived in an old, broken-down house. Every night he used to hear the sound of military drums in the distance. He considered leaving the house, because he was worried about ghosts, but had nowhere else to go. Then one night he dreamt that a messenger from the Golden Elephant kingdom came to him and told him that they were about to go to war against another kingdom, and would appreciate it if he came and watched. Somewhat surprised, he watched as a mouse hole in his house grew to become the gate of a castle, and two great armies marched up outside it.

Once these two armies had assembled, an advisor came up to the Golden Elephant king, offering him the advice that 'The Horse goes diagonally and stops at three, the General moves all over the field, the Chariot proceeds straight into the enemy's territory, and Soldiers should not move sideways.' The King agreed to this plan, but Cen Shun was confused; it did not sound like any battle strategy he had ever heard of. But, the drums sounded and a horse jumped three feet diagonally. The drums sounded again and a soldier marched sideways one foot. The drums sounded a third time and the chariot rolled forward. Following these procedures, the war lasted less than a day, and the other kingdom was badly defeated, forcing the king to flee to the south west. The Golden Elephant kingdom celebrated in style, with drinks being pressed on Cen Shun and assurances that he would still be rich. Then he woke up, still in his cold broken-down house.

He told his family about the dream, and they suggested that he dug up his house, thinking that there might be hidden treasure there. They did so, and found treasure, but not the type they expected. Instead of money or magic, they found a game board with pieces of gold and silver. Cen Shun realized that the advisor had actually been describing how the pieces moved in the game. He sold the board and used the money to set up in business and buy a new, unhaunted house.

These two stories were both probably later inventions to explain the history of the game. The second one seems very close to xiangqi rules, but was likely invented around 839 AD to add a veneer of culture and antiquity to the newly changed game.

The spread of xiangqi

Xiangqi really took off during the Song dynasty, between 960 and 1279 AD. It seems to have become popular quite quickly over all parts of the country, and a few changes to the rules were made, as mentioned earlier. One poem on xiangqi calls it 'the game of the big cities' and says that 'smiling in front of a xiangqi table, even powerful leaders like Liu and Han can fight it out casually'. This seems to suggest it was a game of the urban classes, and other sources show it was popular among the military. There are pictures of Song Emperors playing xiangqi, so it must, we presume, have been popular in court.

A fine set of bronze game pieces from the period has been found, which tells us some interesting things. As well as the normal characters, the pieces also have pictures on the back. The pictures for the Advisors, oddly enough, show female guards holding swords; a very curious flight of fancy. Elephants and Horses look much as you would expect, except that the picture of the Elephant looks rather like an ox – but it is not bad when you consider that the artist must have been working from secondary sources rather than from life. Most curiously of all, the Cannon are shown as catapults, and the Chariots as wagons loaded with rocks for the catapults. This was probably just a little imagination on the part of the artist, as the Chinese certainly had actual – if somewhat unpredictable – cannon, but you cannot help but wonder whether the purpose of the Chariots was, perhaps, mainly for the Cannon to jump?

After the Song were defeated by the Mongols, xiangqi became less popular for a little time, but was soon back to former levels, and has never really stopped since. Collections of games go back to the 14th century and the Ming dynasty, but the Manchu conquerors of 1644, who formed the Qing dynasty, also played the game, attempting to become as Chinese as possible, and the great Manchu emperor Kangxi refers to it in his writings. The 19th century was perhaps the heyday of xiangqi textbooks; there are enough collections of puzzles and game manuals from this period to stop a small army in their own right! Accounts show that they sold extraordinarily well, reflecting, no doubt, the game's huge popularity.

Xiangqi in modern China

Xiangqi is massively popular throughout China, with an estimated two hundred million or more serious players. Virtually every Chinese man knows the rules, and will have played at least one or two games in school. Everywhere you go in China you can see people playing xiangqi, with boards ranging from cheap paper to true antiques, and games can draw quite a crowd of spectators and advisors. If you are travelling in China and you want a game, all you really need to do is take out a board and pieces, and an opponent will present himself pretty quickly.

Like many other aspects of traditional Chinese culture, xiangqi has been absorbed by the Communist government. Mao played the game, reasonably well by all accounts, and the championships, tournaments, and so forth are all state-controlled. As with other sports, mental and physical, children who show strong promise in playing xiangqi are spotted by sports officials and given special fast-track training by the state, and successful players can make a great deal of money, by Chinese standards.

Xiangqi has traditionally been dominated by men, although women have always played, and the author of one Qing text is said to have been female. Normally, women have given up the game when becoming adults, but the Chinese government started strongly to encourage female players in the 1970s in both chess and xiangqi, creating a wave of excellent female xiangqi masters. Currently, championships are still divided by sex, and the women's tournaments receive much less attention than the men's.

As in chess, there is a ranking system, copied from the Western system early this century, with Grandmasters and so forth, and numerous championships, too many to list here, of various importance. The most élite of these is the Five Ram Tournament, open to Grandmasters only. Hu Rong Hua, one of whose games we saw in the previous chapter, is perhaps the greatest living player, and has won 13 national championships. His name has huge cachet in xiangqi circles.

Although still an élite player, he has been eclipsed in the last few years by Grandmaster Lu Qin, a positional genius who currently holds the title of *qi wang* or 'King of Chess', the highest achievable xiangqi title. In 1999 he took both the national championship and the Five Ram Tournament. Recently, he took on the world over the Internet, players all over the world contributing moves for the other side; as of the time of writing, he is winning with ease!

No computer program has yet beaten a xiangqi grandmaster, unlike in chess. This is largely due to the fact that no lab has taken the time to write one yet, though, rather than due to inherent difficulties in xiangqi. It lends itself well, like chess and unlike go, to computer analysis.

Xiangqi internationally

Firstly, I should note that xiangqi is extremely popular all over south-east Asia, and is played particularly widely in Vietnam and Taiwan. It has also become more common in Japan of recent years. Chinese grandmasters dominate, but Taiwan, Vietnam, and Hong Kong have all produced grandmasters. In sheer numbers, xiangqi is far more popular than Western chess.

However, xiangqi has never really taken off in the West. This is odd, considering the fairly wide popularity of wei-chi/go and shogi. I personally suspect that there are two reasons for this: firstly, the popularity of go and shogi owes much to them being widely played in Japan during the Nipponophilia of the 1980s. Secondly, xiangqi is perhaps a little too close to chess to have the foreign appeal that go and shogi do; it can seem more like an interesting variant than a passion in its own right.

There are obviously strong xiangqi societies in Western Chinese communities, but Western players have, until recently, been relatively isolated and had difficulty finding people to play against. However, the rise of the Internet has made it much easier for players to contact and play against each other, and xiangqi is growing in popularity in both Europe and the Americas. There are now xiangqi clubs in almost all countries, easily found over the Internet. Toronto has a particularly well-known club, which produces a great deal of material on the Net.

Xiangqi clubs are generally very sociable, as they will be keen to have a new player. If you have a Chinese cultural centre near you (I know of ones in Manchester and London, at least) you will also find a ready source of opponents there, and a chance to get to know more about the society which produced the game.

Further Information

Unsurprisingly, there are many old texts on xiangqi, and a plethora of modern books on the subject, which can be found in any modern Chinese bookstore. Unfortunately and obviously, they are all in Chinese! This makes them useless for the majority of Westerners, though if the game seizes you to the extent that you go out and learn how to read Chinese, I would be very happy. Often, too, the diagrams are perfectly followable, so if you have a decently sized Chinese community in your area, it is well worth going down and browsing in the local store.

Very little has been written about xiangqi in English, but there are two books worth checking out. Sadly, these are only published in the United States, but they are available via Amazon and other Internet booksellers, and from a couple of the websites mentioned below. Firstly, H. T. Lau's *Chinese Chess*, published by Tuttle in 1991, is a well-illustrated, occasionally slightly clumsy overview of the game, including an analysis of two classic games from 17th-century manuals. *Chinese Chess for Beginners*, published in 1989 by Yutopian Enterprises, is a well-written, quite amusing guide written by a well-travelled American, Sam Sloan. And Midnite Snack, an American games company, produces xiangqi boards suitable for playing while travelling, which are also available through Amazon.

The *Xiangqi Review* is a decent bi-monthly magazine, available by subscription only from David Woo's Chinese Chess Institute, PO Box 5305, Hercules, CA 94547-5305 USA, or by e-mailing dwwoo@juno.com.

The World Wide Web

As with books, there are many more websites on xiangqi in Chinese than in English. Several of the ones that are – supposedly – in English are also given to, to be charitable, somewhat tangled syntax. There is also a news-group: rec.games chinese-chess, but it sees very little traffic nowadays and probably is not worth your time. Some of the best websites are listed below:

http://www.msoworld.com is the homepage of the Mind Sports Olympiads, and has a fantastic xiangqi section, including coverage of recent events, championships, and so forth, and fascinating articles on the game. You can also play xiangqi on-line, and probably, like me, get yourself thrashed by some 12-year-old child prodigy from Shanghai. Well worth a visit, as it is well written and well designed, a rare combination.

http://www.xiangqi.com is a great site for on-line play, as well as hav-ing an extremely good FAQ for the game. Very well crafted, and gives you access to thousands of other players. It also has rather nice interviews and articles.

http://www.beidou-xiangqi.com is an on-line xiangqi magazine based in Singapore, in both Chinese and (good) English. The annotated games, especially those by Hu Rong Hua, are well worth studying, and there are some interesting articles, but you have to pay a subscription fee to get full access.

http://txa.ipoline.com/xq.html is a mainstay for both Chinese and English players. The writing is a little clumsy at times, but there are tons of stuff there, including contact details for xiangqi groups and individual play-ers all over the world. Their collection of games is very large.

http://206.184.157.220/chinesechess is the homepage of Yutopian Enterprises, which specializes in Oriental games. Both the books listed above can be ordered via this page. You can also buy various other xiangqi items, including electronic game boards and the like. There is also a great collection of problems from classical texts on xiangqi, and some rather use-ful fonts for displaying xiangqi games within MSWord

http://i.am or **http://www.geocities.com/TimesSquare/Cave/ 7230/tutorial/menu.html** contains much interesting information, but in rather broken Chinglish. Its Java Applets for displaying games are rather nice, and there are a number of games from recent years stored online. It has a number of good links to other sites.

http://www.hku.hk/acabox/milo/software/mcchess has a good one-player xiangqi computer game you can download, which is reasonably intelligent and plays quite strongly.

On another subject, there are some lovely traditional xiangqi boards available. Your best chance of buying one is probably in Hong Kong, but you might find one in a decently sized Chinatown – I have seen a couple in Manchester and London.

Finally, further information about xiangqi in England is available by writing to

The United Kingdom Chinese Chess Association
12 Lagan House
Sumner Road
London
SE15 5RB
ENGLAND.

Notes

帥 車 炮 馬 兵 將 仕

Notes